PICTORIAL HISTORY
OF THE R.A.F.

PICTORIAL HISTORY OF

THE R.A.F.

Volume 2 . 1939–1945

J. W. R. TAYLOR

AND

P. J. R. MOYES

LONDON

IAN ALLAN

First published 1969

SBN 7110 0055 7

Published by Ian Allan Ltd., Terminal House, Shepperton, Surrey, and printed in the
United Kingdom by R. J. Acford Ltd., Industrial Estate, Chichester, Sussex

Contents

Introduction

The author of one popular history of the Battle of Britain has expressed the opinion that the battle was lost by the *Luftwaffe* rather than won by the Royal Air Force. Those of us privileged to have lived through the Summer months of 1940, in England, can feel only contempt for such triviality. Here was one of the decisive battles in history, which ended with the *Luftwaffe* driven from the daylight skies over Britain by the numerically-inferior squadrons of R.A.F. Fighter Command. From that moment, however grim the struggle, defeat was unthinkable for the British people.

Five more years were to pass before the enemy was crushed. In those years, the Royal Air Force flew and fought everywhere from the snows of Northern Russia to the deserts of North Africa, from the solitude of mid-Atlantic to the too-full skies over the Ruhr. No single volume could contain details of each important action or even every aspect of an air war as widespread and complex as this. What we have tried to do in this small book is to trace briefly the main course of the war in the air in each theatre, to tell how it was fought, with what and by whom, and to explain why campaigns worked out as they did.

The reader may look in vain for particular deeds of individual heroism or for a reference to the service record of an obscure type of aircraft flown briefly by one or two squadrons. It is our hope that he will not look in vain for the reason why historians of the future will regard this period as the British Empire's finest hour, and that he will learn in truth the greatness of the part that the Royal Air Force played in making final victory possible.

January, 1969   J.W.R.T. and P.J.R.M.

Chapter One

Europe: September 1939 - June 1940

We shall fight in France, we shall fight in the seas and oceans, we shall fight with growing confidence and growing strength in the air; we shall defend our Island whatever the cost may be. We shall fight on the beaches, we shall fight on the landing-grounds, we shall fight in the fields and in the streets, we shall fight in the hills; we shall never surrender.

Winston Churchill: June 4th, 1940

ONLY IN THE opening minutes of World War II did the people of Britain display their fear. The Prime Minister, Neville Chamberlain, had barely finished his radio broadcast, announcing that Britain was at war with Germany, when the sirens wailed their warning of impending air attack. Knowing what destruction the *Luftwaffe* had caused to open cities in Spain, the citizens of London fled for shelter; but it was a false alarm, caused by faulty identification of a friendly civil aircraft. By the time the real attacks came, the men and women had learned the limitations as well as the destructive power of aerial bombardment and were able to face up to it.

The year of grace gained, unwittingly, by the Munich Agreement had not been wasted. If the *Luftwaffe* had despatched its full force of 1,200 long-range bombers against Britain in September 1938, R.A.F. Fighter Command would have had only 93 modern monoplane fighters and 573 obsolescent biplanes with which to oppose them. No Spitfires were operational by then and the Hurricanes, without gun heating, were unable to fight above 15,000 feet.

By September 3rd, 1939, the situation was very different. Sir Hugh Dowding, Air Officer Commanding-in-Chief of Fighter Command, was still far short of the 53 squadrons considered essential for the defence of the United Kingdom, but the 35 squadrons at his disposal included 22 equipped with Hurricanes and Spitfires. He begrudged the four squadrons of Hurricanes sent to France to provide air cover for the British Expeditionary Force, and he bitterly opposed every attempt to drain away his resources, such as the suggestion that his units could be made mobile, defending the B.E.F. one day and re-crossing the Channel next day, if necessary, to intercept *Luftwaffe* raiders over Britain.

In retrospect, it is clear that Dowding's single-mindedness saved Britain when the air assault came in the Summer of 1940. At the time, his colleagues in the other Commands and Services felt only resentment when he expressed his view that 'the home defence organisation must not be regarded as co-equal with other Commands, but should receive priority to all other claims until it is firmly secured, since the continued existence of the nation, and of its Services, depends on the Royal Navy and Fighter Command'.

With fewer than 100 Hurricanes and Spitfires a month leaving the assembly lines, Dowding was told that the only additions to his force that he could expect immediately were two squadrons equipped with a fighter version of the Blenheim. He asked instead for four half-squadrons, which could be expanded to full strength later. At the same time, he transformed one training squadron into two operational half-squadrons and asked Sir Cyril Newall, Chief of Air Staff, to allocate two more as an insurance against any of his squadrons being sent to France.

Newall did better than this. At an Air Staff meeting on October 17th, 1939, he said that not only must the eight projected half-squadrons be formed by the end of the month, but that another ten had to follow by mid-November. He did not say how this was to be achieved. Nevertheless, Dowding had his 18 embryo fighter squadrons by December, equipped for the most part with Blenheims, but some having to make do with aging Battle day-bombers. Fortunately, they were not called upon to fly into action with such unsuitable aircraft. By the time the real shooting war started in the Spring of 1940, half of them had re-equipped with Hurricanes and Spitfires—giving Dowding 38 monoplane squadrons in a total of 47, after losing four Blenheim squadrons to Costal Command and two mobile squadrons to the B.E.F.

Unfortunately, Dowding's belief that squadrons sent to France were as good as lost proved only too true, as did his conviction that the fate of Britain would be decided ultimately in air battles over these islands.

Bearing in mind the lateness with which Britain had started its massive re-armament programme in the mid-thirties, our defences were at a surprisingly high state of readiness when war came. When, for example, the ten squadrons of Battle day-bombers which made up the Advanced Air Striking Force flew to their operational bases in the Rheims area of France on September 2nd, the eve of war, they were able to prepare for action immediately by loading bombs laid down some time earlier under the guise of a sale to the French Air Force.

The A.A.S.F. formed one branch of the British Air Forces in France, Commanded by Air Marshal A. S. Barratt. The other branch was the Air Component, intended solely to provide support for the Army, with five squadrons of Lysanders for tactical and photographic reconnaissance and four squadrons of Hurricanes for escort, interception and ground attack duties. Two further squadrons of Hurricanes (increased soon to four) were allocated to the A.A.S.F.

As its name implied, the A.A.S.F. was intended originally as the forward-based element of the R.A.F.'s strategic attack force, based so close to Germany that even its short-range day bombers would be able to deal heavy blows against enemy airfields and industry. In the event, it never operated in this way.

During the period of the so-called 'phoney' war, it was the deliberate policy of the British government to avoid using the R.A.F. in any way that would provoke German retaliation against this country. This was not merely an expression of the hope that the worst horrors of modern war might still be averted—as the Germans also showed no eagerness to exchange blows with Britain and France after polishing off Poland in a brutal, professionally-executed 28-day *blitzkrieg* (lightning war)—but also an opportunity to build up our strength at a time when military production was beginning to reach really healthy proportions.

The initial task allocated to the A.A.S.F. squadrons was, therefore, reconnaissance to a depth of some 10 or 20 miles over the Franco-German border. It lasted precisely one month. On September 30th, five Battles of No. 150 Squadron were pounced on by Bf 109 fighters. Four were shot down, the fifth damaged beyond repair, and the Battle's career as a strategic bomber was over before it started. Plans were made to replace it with the Blenheim, but the process had hardly begun when the A.A.S.F. ceased to exist.

Few people should have been surprised by the discovery that the Battle was by then a virtual death-trap for its crews. The prototype was ordered under Specification P.27/32, in 1932, only as an experiment, to discover how a cleanly-designed single-engined bomber would compare with the twin-engined Wellington and Hampden built to Specification B.9/32. It was clear from the start that it lacked the performance and defensive capability of the twins; but so great was the need to produce large numbers of new combat aircraft quickly under the expansion programme that no fewer than 2,196 were eventually delivered. The A.A.S.F. was the force unlucky enough to have to match the Battle's top speed of 241 m.p.h. and armament of one fixed and one movable machine-gun against 354 m.p.h. Bf 109E fighters armed with two 20-mm. cannon and two machine-guns.

The vulnerability of the Battle was not the only disagreeable lesson learned by the R.A.F. in the early stages of the war. Equally worrying were the early experiences of Bomber Command, which compelled its A.O.C.-in-C., Air Chief Marshal Sir Edgar Ludlow-Hewitt, to make drastic changes in its operational techniques.

On paper, he had 55 squadrons in the Summer of 1939; but the total of 480 aircraft was spread too thinly so, by the end of September, Bomber Command had been trimmed to 33 front-line squadrons, of which ten were in France as the A.A.S.F. Those remaining in Britain were all rather better equipped, with twin-engined bombers. No. 2 Group, for example, based in East Anglia, had six squadrons of Mk. IV Blenheims. These had a shorter range than other home-based bombers (1,460 miles with 1,000 lb. of bombs), but their maximum speed of 266 m.p.h. and defensive armament of up to five machine-guns gave them a fighting chance in combat.

The second East Anglian group, No. 3, had six squadrons of Wellington I and IA aircraft, with a range of 1,200 miles carrying 4,500 lb. of bombs or 2,550 miles with 1,000 lb. Among the attractions of the Wellington were its immensely strong 'basket-work' geodetic construction, devised by the great Barnes Wallis, and its heavy armament of six machine-guns—four of them in power-operated turrets.

The Wellington was to prove good enough to remain in front-line service throughout the war, equipping no fewer than 21 squadrons of Bomber Command and many others in Coastal Command at its peak deployment in 1942. Its maximum speed of 235–255 m.p.h. was greatly envied by crews of the five squadrons of No. 4 Group in Yorkshire, whose lumbering Whitley IIIs and IVs normally plodded along at a sedate 185 m.p.h. Even when fitted with a four-gun tail turret, the Whitley was clearly a sitting duck in daylight; so it was able to be used only at night, whereas the rest of Bomber Command was expected to operate mainly by day.

Last of the four home-based Groups was No. 5, with six squadrons of Hampdens, based in Lincolnshire. Although quite fast, with a top speed of 254 m.p.h., and able to carry 1,885 lb. of bombs for 2,000 miles, the Hampden had features which lessened its popularity. In particular, the slim fuselage was very cramped for the crew and its guns were not mounted in turrets, with the result that the gunners had a number of blind spots which the aircraft's excellent manoeuvrability could only partially offset.

From its birth the R.A.F. had been brought up on the philosophy that victory in war can be achieved most economically by heavy and sustained air attacks on the enemy. Within the restrictions imposed by the government's policy, Bomber Command did its best to put that theory into practice.

One of its primary, and permitted, tasks was to support the Navy by keeping track of German fleet movements. In this it did not have to start from scratch. During the nine months prior to the outbreak of war, a pale green twin-engined Lockheed 12A transport owned by an Australian named Sidney Cotton was a familiar sight over Germany. The Berlin agent for his colour-film business had served with Reichsmarschall Hermann Goering in the Richthofen squadron in 1918, and introduced Cotton to senior *Luftwaffe* officers, who were soon competing for joyrides in the Lockheed. As they flew to and from beauty spots on the Rhine, the Germans were unaware that a panel had slid back to permit three reconnaissance cameras mounted in the aircraft's belly to photograph airfields, factories, military installations and anything else of interest. When asked why his flights between London and Berlin sometimes took him near the naval base at Wilhelmshaven, Cotton replied that, like Lindbergh, he always flew a great circle route.

Thanks to photographs taken by Cotton and his colleague, Bob Niven, the British Chiefs of Staff knew exactly which units of the enemy fleet were at Wilhelmshaven on September 2nd, 1939. Less than an hour after war was declared, a Blenheim of No. 139 Squadron, piloted by Flying Officer A. McPherson, took off from Wyton, in Huntingdonshire, to see if they were still there. From a height of 24,000 feet, McPherson and the naval observer who was his passenger saw several heavy warships moving out into the Schillig Roads. Unfortunately, their radio froze up in the intense cold and they could not pass on the news until they landed back at

Wyton. By then it was too late in the afternoon for a strike force of day bombers to take off.

When McPherson repeated his reconnaissance flight next morning, bad weather forced him down to 300 feet over the German naval bases. Again his radio failed and two more hours were lost when he returned, as his report made it necessary to change for the fourth time the type of bombs fitted to the 15 Blenheims of Nos. 107 and 110 Squadrons at Wattisham and No. 139 Squadron at Wyton, which had been standing by for two days.

Led by Flt. Lt. K. C. Doran, the Wattisham squadrons made their attacks in a shallow dive from 500 feet. Although caught unawares, the Germans soon got their ship and shore-based anti-aircraft guns into action and one aircraft of No. 110 Squadron and four of the five from No. 107 failed to return. The battleship *Admiral von Scheer* was hit by several 500-lb. bombs but, being set with an 11-second-delay fuse, they simply bounced off her armoured decks. The only real damage was caused by a crippled Blenheim which crashed into the cruiser *Emden*, killing and injuring many of the German crew. No. 139 Squadron could not even find Wilhelmshaven.

Radio that didn't work, bombs that did no real damage and the difficulty of finding the target in bad weather were only three of the problems presented to Ludlow-Hewitt. On the same day, two of the 14 Wellingtons from Nos. 9 and 149 Squadrons that attacked the naval base of Brunsbüttel failed to return—with little to show on the credit side—as only one crew claimed even a possible hit on a ship.

It was decided that future attacks should be made only against ships at sea. This reflected both the proven high cost of flying over heavily-defended bases and a wish to avoid civilian casualties at a time when the *Luftwaffe* was showing no eagerness to attack the United Kingdom. The trouble was that by the time a bomber force reached the area where ships had been spotted the enemy were usually back in port.

Bomber Command's answer to this was armed reconnaissance in force. On September 29th, eleven Hampdens, in two sections, found and attacked two enemy destroyers near Heligoland, but were intercepted by fighters from the North Frisian Islands and lost five of their number.

By mid-November, the First Lord of the Admiralty, Winston Churchill, was growing impatient over the lack of any major success against the German fleet, at a time when British losses to enemy

U-boats and magnetic mines were mounting. Orders were issued that the R.A.F. should take the first opportunity of carrying out a high-altitude attack with at least 24 aircraft on an important enemy warship in the waters near Wilhelmshaven or Heligoland. Good weather was essential, to avoid any possibility of stray bombs falling on civilians.

The attack was made by 24 Wellingtons of Nos. 38, 115 and 149 Squadrons, on December 3rd. What they did not know was that the Germans, as well as Britain, had early-warning radar, and the anti-aircraft gunners at Heligoland were waiting for them. The broken cloud over the enemy ships, which hampered the bomb-aimers in the aircraft, also prevented the enemy *flak* from achieving any success. On balance, the Wellington crews came out best, with one German minesweeper sunk by a bomb that passed right through it without exploding and one enemy fighter shot down at no cost to the R.A.F.

It was believed that this modest success proved the ability of a bomber force to operate unescorted in daylight, without too much danger, provided it maintained formation, so that the gunners could protect it with heavy cross-fire. Disillusionment came swiftly. On December 14th, 12 Wellingtons of No. 99 Squadron came under heavy attack from enemy fighters and anti-aircraft guns over the Schillig Roads and lost half their number. None of the missing aircraft was believed to have fallen to *Luftwaffe* fighters, but any remaining confidence was shattered four days later when 22 Wellingtons from Nos. 9, 37 and 149 Squadrons found Bf 109s and Me 110s waiting for them in great strength.

No bombs could be dropped, as all enemy ships sighted were in harbour, where an attack might have led to civilian casualties. In contrast, ten Wellingtons were shot down, two more had to ditch in the sea and three others were lost in forced-landings.

The success of its radar-alerted fighters ought to have served as a warning to the *Luftwaffe* of the kind of reception it would receive if it ever ventured in force over Britain. In the event, Bomber Command seems to have been quickest to learn.

Most of the Wellingtons were lost to beam attacks from above and were last seen in flames or with petrol pouring from their punctured fuel tanks. Plans were made immediately to fit beam machine-guns, self-sealing fuel tanks and extra armour plate. Even more important, the policy of despatching Wellingtons and Hampdens over Germany by day was abandoned.

To the disgust of their crews, the Whitleys had always been

restricted to night operations. This meant that, instead of bombs, they were permitted to drop on Germany only propaganda leaflets. The long endurance of the Whitleys enabled them to range as far as Vienna, Prague, Berlin, and even Warsaw on their pamphlet raids, known officially as 'Nickels'. Losses, inevitably, were high, amounting to some six per cent of the total sorties made in the first seven months of the war. In terms of direct results, this was completely unjustified; but from the experiences of the crews who flew these first large-scale night operations came improvements in navigation aids, emergency drill and equipment for high flying. Their observations of such things as activity at enemy airfields and the location of anti-aircraft defences and dummy towns were also of great value later.

Bad weather and the cold at high altitude caused many of the losses. One crew, returning from Munich, could not retract the 'dustbin' lower turret through which they had dropped their leaflets. Then a cylinder head blew off the starboard engine and the Whitley began sinking through heavy snow clouds. The pilot ordered the crew to take to their parachutes, finally jumping himself. The aircraft continued down in a gentle glide, bumped to a halt on the ground and burst into flames. The rear gunner, who had not heard the order to bale out, left his turret and dashed round to the front to see if his colleagues were safe. He found them eventually in a café in a nearby village and is said to have invented some new words when he had used up his normal vocabulary in describing what he thought of them!

Another Whitley crew, running short of fuel, landed as soon as they felt they were safely across the Franco-German border. When they heard the group of locals who had come to inspect the aircraft talking in German, they realised their mistake and just managed to take off again as a party of enemy troops arrived on the scene.

While Bomber Command tried, without much success, to reduce Germany's sea power and Fighter Command waited for an enemy who did not come, Coastal Command was engaged in a life and death struggle from the first day of the war. For the second time this century, the Germans decided that the easiest way to defeat Britain was to cut her sea supply routes and so starve both her industry and her people into submission.

When the Fleet Air Arm had passed back to Admiralty control in 1937, Coastal Command had been retained by the R.A.F.; but it worked closely with the Royal Navy, and the Area Combined

Headquarters of each of its three Groups was staffed jointly by air and naval officers.

It was less well-equipped than other Commands, partly through the deliberate and logical policy of giving priority to our strategic attack and defence forces, but also because it was felt that the might of the Royal Navy and its allies provided an adequate shield against anything that the German fleet might attempt. This over-confidence might have proved fatal at the height of the U-boat campaign but for the courage of those who fought the Battle of the Atlantic under Allied colours, both military and civilian.

Standard maritime reconnaissance aircraft, with eleven out of twelve Coastal squadrons, was the twin-engined Anson. No aeroplane was ever more reliable; but 'faithful Annie', as the aircraft was known to its crews, had a maximum speed of only 188 m.p.h., an armament of only one fixed machine-gun and another in a dorsal turret, a normal radius of action of about 250 miles and an offensive load of 100-lb. anti-submarine bombs that were of little use against contemporary submarines.

In one respect, the inadequacy of our bombs was a god-send. Two days after the war started, Ansons attacked by mistake two Royal Navy submarines, which suffered nothing worse than a slight shaking. In a similar incident on December 3rd, H.M. Submarine *Snapper* received a direct hit by a 100-lb. bomb at the base of her conning tower and lost four electric light bulbs in her control room.

The remaining reconnaissance squadron had the first of an initial batch of 200 Hudsons ordered from America in 1938. At the time, the order had caused such an outcry from people who believed that the R.A.F. should 'buy British' that it was intended to use the aircraft primarily as navigation trainers. In fact, the Ansons were switched to training just as quickly as they could be replaced by the faster and more effective Hudsons.

The American aircraft soon made their mark. On October 8th one of them, serving with No. 224 Squadron, became the first home-based R.A.F. aircraft to destroy an enemy aeroplane when its crew brought down a Dornier Do 18 flying-boat over the North Sea. Four months later, a Hudson of No. 220 Squadron directed Royal Naval forces to where the German prison ship *Altmark* was hiding in Norwegian waters and so brought freedom to many captured British seamen.

Hudsons were also the first Coastal Command aircraft to be fitted with ASV (air-to-surface-vessel) radar, for hunting enemy ships and surfaced submarines at night, in the first weeks of 1940.

The other great mainstay of Coastal Command from the start
of World War II was the Sunderland. Only three of the six flying-
boat squadrons had been re-equipped with this fine four-engined
aircraft by the outbreak of war, but the others soon traded their
Londons and Stranraers for Sunderlands. They quickly showed
their capabilities, in actions typical of those that were to be carried
out by flying-boat squadrons throughout the entire war, in every
theatre.

The war was only 15 days old when two Sunderlands from Nos. 204
and 228 Squadrons picked up distress signals from the tramp steamer
Kensington Court, torpedoed by a U-boat some 70 miles off the
Scillies. Alighting in the rough sea, the flying-boats picked up the
entire crew of 34, who were back on shore within an hour of being
attacked.

A Sunderland of No. 228 Squadron avenged the *Kensington Court*
on January 31st, 1940, when the crew of *U-55*, already damaged by
surface forces, scuttled their submarine on being sighted by the
flying-boat—the first of many U-boats to fall victim to Coastal
Command, although most of the others put up more of a fight.

With its armament of one machine-gun in a power-operated bow
turret, four in a tail turret and two in beam positions, the Sunderland
was well able to take care of itself in air combat. This was proved
for the first time on April 3rd, 1940, when six Ju 88 twin-engined
fighters pounced on a lone Sunderland over the North Sea. After
one Ju 88 had gone down in flames and another had limped off to
a forced landing in Norway, the rest decided to call it a day. From
then on, the *Luftwaffe* referred respectfully to this British aircraft as
the 'Flying Porcupine'.

Main tasks of Coastal Command were to search for, report and
destroy enemy ships, but every week seemed to bring new demands
on its small, inadequately-equipped force. Four squadrons of
Blenheim IVs were added to its strength, each fitted with an under-
belly pack of four machine-guns, to supplement Fighter Command
in the work of providing protection for East Coast convoys and
mine-layers.

When magnetic mines were added to the menace of the U-boats,
Coastal Command received its first Wellingtons, each fitted with a
huge metal ring containing a magnetic coil. Flying very low over
the sea, these aircraft exploded one-eighth of all the magnetic mines
rendered harmless between November 1939 and May 1940, at no
small risk to their crews.

To offset its shortage of aircraft, Coastal Command formed flights of unarmed Tiger Moth and Hornet Moth lightplanes to fly over the sea at night, in the belief that the sound of any aero-engine would cause mine-laying U-boats to suspend their work and submerge. The Admiralty also tried briefly to augment the Command's efforts by using aircraft carriers to protect convoys beyond the range of the Ansons and Sunderlands. The prompt loss of H.M.S. *Courageous* in the Bristol Channel, and narrow escape of H.M.S. *Ark Royal*, soon ended this experiment.

Except at sea, the war was very different to that which everyone had expected; but no-one doubted that the storm would break eventually and the Air Ministry made good use of the period of comparative calm. The formation of new squadrons and the re-equipment of existing squadrons proceeded with fresh urgency. The first specialised photographic reconnaissance unit was brought into being at Heston aerodrome, under the leadership of Sidney Cotton, by now a slightly reluctant Squadron Leader, and eventually managed to wheedle out of the Air Ministry two precious Spitfires as well as some Blenheims. Behind the scenes, a whole new generation of combat aircraft began to take shape, including an unorthodox —and largely unwanted—all-wooden unarmed high-speed bomber known as the Mosquito, for which the de Havilland company managed to gain official support, thanks to the personal enthusiasm of Sir Wilfred Freeman, Member for Research, Development and Production on the Air Council.

Even more important, the birth of the great Empire Air Training Scheme, on December 17th, 1939, ensured the future availability of finely trained men to fly the new aircraft. Canada agreed to create 13 Elementary Flying Training Schools, 16 Service Flying Training Schools, 10 Air Observer Schools, 10 Bombing and Gunnery Schools and two Air Navigation Schools, mainly for volunteers from Canada, Australia and New Zealand, but with some pupils from the U.K. Australia promised nine Elementary and seven Service Flying Training Schools, four Air Observer and four Bombing and Gunnery Schools for her own citizens. New Zealand offered to contribute three Elementary and two Service Flying Training Schools for New Zealanders.

These schools, operating under the peaceful skies of the Commonwealth, were expected to produce an annual total of 11,000 pilots and 17,000 other aircrew by mid-1942. In fact, they bettered this, and were supplemented by many schools for R.A.F. aircrew in Southern Rhodesia and South Africa.

The first courses under the Empire Air Training Scheme began on April 19th, 1940. By then, the 'phoney' war was over and one of the most desperate, action-packed five-month periods in British history had begun.

It was preceded by characteristic dilly-dallying and indecision by the British War Cabinet of the time. With two-thirds of all Germany's supplies of iron ore coming from Sweden and Norway—one-third of these imports travelling via Norwegian territorial waters—it would clearly have been profitable to base British forces in Scandinavia. The war between Russia and Finland offered sufficient excuse, and a large three-Service force was gathered together to go to the aid of the Finns. Before it could be despatched, the Finns sued for peace. It was decided, instead, to mine the Norwegian waters through which the ore-ships passed to Germany. Again characteristically, Britain warned Norway and Sweden that this was to be done, on April 5th, 1940. Two days earlier, without any warning, the first ships of a German invasion force had put to sea to forestall any possible allied presence in Norway.

By April 12th, Denmark had been occupied by the Germans almost without effort and Norway was as good as won. Powerful army units were in possession of most key points in the country, with nearly 600 combat aircraft and more than 600 transport aircraft to support them. The German Navy had suffered some heavy losses at the hands of the Royal Navy, but had done its job well. German sympathisers in the country had done their traitorous work and the name of their leader, Vidkun Quisling, had become a synonym for those willing to betray their homeland.

Every Norwegian port and airfield of any consequence was in enemy hands, but it was decided to fight back. British and French troops were landed at Namsos and Aandalsnes, with the object of converging on Trondheim. It was soon clear that, without air support, they would be destroyed by the *Luftwaffe*. Led by a Fleet Air Arm Skua, the 18 Gladiator biplanes of No. 263 Squadron, under Sqn. Ldr. J. W. Donaldson, took off from H.M.S. *Glorious*, 180 miles from the Norwegian coast, in a heavy snowstorm and landed on the frozen Lake Lesjaskog that was to be their base. The remains of one of them can still be seen there.

The destruction of No. 263 Squadron began early on the morning of April 25th, within hours of its arrival. After two hours of backbreaking, heartbreaking effort had unfrozen their carburettors and controls, and freed the tyres from ice that welded them to the surface of the lake and their own axles, two Gladiators had become airborne and were putting fresh heart into British troops who had, until then, seen only aircraft painted with swastikas and black crosses. But by 7 a.m., the *Luftwaffe* was also over Lake Lesjaskog—in force.

Between bombing raids by Ju 88s and He 111s, No. 263 finally got all its Gladiators into the air. An He 115 seaplane had been destroyed by the first patrol at 5 a.m. An He 111 was shot down at 9.15 a.m., followed by a second at mid-day. By then, however, ten Gladiators had been wrecked on the ground.

When night fell, only four Gladiators were still airworthy. Next day, one suffered an engine failure and its pilot had to take to his parachute. The remaining three were destroyed by the Squadron when it was ordered home on the 28th, with all its fuel and all chance of further combat gone. If courage alone had been sufficient for victory, No. 263 could have taken on the whole *Luftwaffe*. Its official tally of 14 enemy aircraft destroyed was achieved without the loss of a single Gladiator in air combat.

Almost unbelievably, No. 263 was back in Norway on May 22nd, based at Bardufoss in the far north, in support of the British forces at Narvik. Fighting side-by-side with No. 46 (Hurricane) Squadron, it managed to establish local air superiority while the soldiers captured and destroyed Narvik, ending with 36 more enemy aircraft to its credit.

Events in France had by then compelled a decision to leave Norway to its fate. The Gladiators were flown on to H.M.S. *Glorious*; the Hurricanes were to have been destroyed but, realising how valuable such aircraft might be in the months ahead, their pilots begged to be allowed to follow the old biplanes on to the ship, although none of them had ever before made a deck landing and it had always been considered out of the question to fly such high-performance aircraft on to carriers—particularly without a deck arrester hook. Every pilot landed successfully. All but two died when *Glorious* was sunk by the battle cruisers *Scharnhorst* and *Gneisenau* on its way back to Britain.

Norway had been gained for Hitler largely by the action of the *Luftwaffe*, operating beyond the effective range of R.A.F. bombers. What would have seemed even more unbelievable a few weeks earlier is that, only one week after the *Glorious* was sunk, on June 8th, Belgium, Holland and France were also defeated and Mussolini had decided that, as the war appeared to be over, Italy would lose little by coming in on Germany's side in time to share the spoils.

Once again, the R.A.F. had done all that could have been expected of it, and more, in the face of the overwhelming might of Germany's *blitzkreig* tactics and at the side of an ill-prepared ally. Following its nationalisation in 1936, the French aircraft industry had gone to pieces. First-class designs flew as prototypes, but production was a shambles. In particular, the French Air Force could muster fewer than 100 bombers, of which only 25 were modern. Even worse, our allies were so frightened of the *Luftwaffe* that on more than one occasion they prevented R.A.F. bombers from taking off in France for fear that this might provoke reprisals against French cities.

The German onslaught began on May 10th. As expected, the main thrusts were through Holland, Belgium and Luxembourg rather than against the Maginot Line. Seventy airfields in France, Belgium and the Netherlands came under heavy *Luftwaffe* attack, but R.A.F. squadrons suffered little from this initial offensive and the Hurricanes were soon taking tremendous toll of the enemy, while Blenheims tried to pin-point the movements of enemy ground forces.

Because of their known vulnerability to fighter attack, the Battles of the A.A.S.F. were ordered to approach their targets at 250 feet when despatched to bomb advancing columns of enemy troops. They flew into a wall of fire from the ground and by nightfall on the first day 13 of the 32 Battles sent into action had been lost. Worse was to follow.

On May 11th, eight Battles from Nos. 88 and 218 Squadrons attacked a troop column in Germany. More precisely, they were *sent* to attack it; the only pilot to return was doubtful if any crew reached their target. On the same day, No. 114 (Blenheim) Squadron was all but wiped out on its airfield, and on the 12th the other A.A.S.F. Blenheim squadron (No. 139) lost seven of its nine aircraft when they ran into a swarm of enemy fighters.

In one of the bravest actions of the entire campaign, five crews from No. 12 Squadron flew to virtually certain death in their Battles on May 10th, in an attempt to deprive the Germans of two captured bridges at Maastricht. None returned, but one bridge was put out of action and the leader of the raid, Flying Officer D. E. Garland, and his observer, ex-Halton apprentice Sgt. T. Gray, received posthumously the first Victoria Crosses awarded to the R.A.F. in World War II.

In three days, the strength of the A.A.S.F. bomber squadrons had been depleted from 135 to 72. On 14th May, the survivors were called upon for one final all-out effort to try to halt the enemy forces massed for the break-through at Sedan. Out of 71 aircraft from Nos. 12, 103, 105, 139, 150 and 218 Squadrons which took part in the attack, only 40 returned—the highest loss ever experienced by the R.A.F. in an operation on such a scale. When 28 Blenheims of Bomber Command followed the Battles in the evening, they lost seven of their number.

Had those who controlled Britain's armed forces harkened to desperate appeals from across the Channel and flung Bomber and Fighter Commands into daylight support of a campaign already lost, hopelessly, on the ground, the R.A.F. would have been so badly mauled that it could not have saved Britain from invasion. The fact that these Commands were not so committed has led sometimes to the accusation that they left their colleagues at the mercy of the enemy, but this is a travesty of the true facts. The Dunkirk evacuation that snatched survival, if not victory, from defeat, was achieved at high cost to the R.A.F.

Even the Battles of the A.A.S.F. did not give up the fight until resistance in France ended, but they operated by night and suffered only light casualties. Daylight attacks on the German armies advancing to the Channel coast were made mainly by Blenheims, supported sometimes by Lysanders and ancient Hector biplanes, and with an escort of Hurricanes.

Dowding was forced to part with some of his precious Hurricane squadrons, to the extent that the equivalent of 13 squadrons of these aircraft operated eventually with the Air Component. By the time they were evacuated on May 21st, only 66 of the total of 261 sent to France could be flown over the Channel. In ten days, about 25 per cent of the R.A.F.'s total strength in modern fighters had been lost.

Some 200 Hurricanes and Spitfires of Fighter Command helped to cover the evacuation of the B.E.F. from Dunkirk. Hitler had decided to let the *Luftwaffe*, rather than his armies, deal the *coup de grace* to the British troops and in this he made his greatest mistake. The R.A.F. pilots flew with such determination that the enemy often jettisoned his bombs and ran rather than face them. But, inevitably, many German bombers got through, many ships were sunk and many were the tired, frustrated soldiers who asked bitterly 'Where was the R.A.F.?', not seeing the air battles fought behind the beaches.

During the nine days of the evacuation, the R.A.F. flew 651 bomber sorties, 171 reconnaissance sorties and 2,739 fighter sorties in direct support of the operation, while Coastal Command aircraft patrolled skies packed with enemy fighters to keep watch for enemy surface craft and submarines which might have caused havoc among the small unarmed ships that helped to bring the soldiers home.

The operations of May and June 1940 cost the R.A.F. a total of 959 aircraft, from every operational Command, including no fewer than 432 Hurricanes and Spitfires. It will never be known how many of the 1,284 aircraft lost by the *Luftwaffe* fell to the R.A.F., but the proportion must have been high and it was not without reason that Britain's new Prime Minister, Winston Churchill, was able to claim after Dunkirk that 'there was a victory inside this deliverance which should be noted. It was gained by the Royal Air Force'.

Had too high a price been paid for this modest victory? The people of Britain could only wait and see, and pray that it had not been too high, as they prepared to answer their great leader's call to fight on the beaches, on the landing-grounds, in the fields and in the streets—and never to surrender.

Chapter Two

Battle of Britain
June 1940 - October 1940

The Battle of France is over. I expect that the Battle of Britain is about to begin. Upon this battle depends the survival of Christian civilisation. Let us therefore brace ourselves to our duties, and so bear ourselves that, if the British Empire and its Commonwealth last for a thousand years, men will still say: 'This was their finest hour'.

Winston Churchill, June 18th, 1940

THE OPINION OF French military leaders was that, following their defeat by Germany: 'In three weeks England will have her neck wrung like a chicken.' Joseph Kennedy, U.S. Ambassador in London, was of much the same opinion. Ex-German Ambassador von Ribbentrop told the Italians: 'English territorial defence is non-existent. A single German division will suffice to bring about a complete collapse.' On July 16th, Hitler issued a directive stating: 'Since England in spite of her militarily hopeless position shows no sign of coming to terms, I have decided to prepare a landing operation against Britain, and if necessary to carry it out . . . The preparations for the entire operation must be completed by mid-August.' It was to be called Operation Sea Lion.

An armada of 168 transport ships, totalling 700,000 tons, 1,910 barges, 419 tugs and trawlers and 1,600 motor-boats was requisitioned to carry the German army across the narrow seas between France and the coasts of Kent and Sussex. Few of Germany's military leaders relished the thought of penetrating waters dominated by the Royal Navy, but they considered it possible provided the *Luftwaffe* could offer air supremacy above the Channel and the invasion beaches. The first essential was, therefore, to destroy the Royal Air Force and its bases.

So far, little attempt had been made to test in force the effectiveness of Britain's defences. Like Bomber Command, the *Luftwaffe* was restricted initially to attacks on naval targets. Goering wanted to do the job properly by hurling his entire bomber force against the Home Fleet. Had he done so, it might have changed the course of history, for the Royal Navy's main base at Scapa Flow, in the Orkneys, was without any fighter protection at the outbreak of war.

Rosyth was better defended and when ships in the Firth of Forth became the targets of the first air raid on Britain in World War II, on October 16th, 1939, they were defended by Auxiliary Air Force Hurricanes and Gladiators. Damage and casualties were suffered by H.M.S. *Southampton*, *Edinburgh* and *Mohawk*; but the major success scored by the *Luftwaffe* was that, after a further raid on Scapa Flow, the Admiralty decided to move the Home Fleet to safer anchorage in the Clyde, thereby reducing considerably its effectiveness against any German raider that might break out into the Atlantic or any force sent against Britain's East Coast. It did so at the cost of only four aircraft; but, as so often happened, the Germans failed to take advantage of the strategic gain they had won.

By the time the Fleet returned to Scapa Flow in March 1940, the base was defended by three Hurricane squadrons at Wick, a squadron of 56 barrage balloons and early warning radar. An He 111 that probed the defences was promptly shot down by No. 111 Squadron. On March 16th, the enemy managed to elude the defences, damaging H.M.S. *Norfolk* and *Iron Duke* and bombing the airfield at Hatston without loss. They also caused the first civilian deaths in a World War II air raid by dropping bombs on the island of Hoy. In retaliation, the War Cabinet ordered an attack on the enemy seaplane hangars and slipways at Hornum—the first British raid on a shore base. More important, the incident put the defences on their toes and three subsequent attacks on Scapa Flow were broken up before they could do any damage.

With similar attacks on convoys at sea, that was about the limit of *Luftwaffe* air activities against Britain in the months before Norway was invaded. It cost the enemy about 10 per cent of the 400 aircraft involved, despite the widely-dispersed nature of the raids, in areas where radar coverage and fighter defences were thinly spread. There was, therefore, some excuse for confidence as Britain awaited the German onslaught in mid-1940—although it was, perhaps, as well that the ordinary man and woman in the street did not know the full extent of the threat.

For its *Adlerangriff* (Eagle attack) that would—it was expected—dispose of the R.A.F. as easily as Poland and France had been eliminated, the *Luftwaffe* massed three great *Luftflotten* (Air Fleets), with a total of around 3,500 aircraft. *Luftflotte* 2, led by General Kesselring, was based in the Netherlands, Belgium and north-eastern France. *Luftflotte* 3, under General Sperrle, was in northern and north-western France. *Luftflotte* 5, under General Stumpff was poised to strike from Norway and Denmark.

Against their first-line strength of at least 1,000 long-range bombers, 250 dive-bombers and 1,000 fighters, the R.A.F. could have put up only 331 serviceable Hurricanes and Spitfires and 115 other fighters in early June 1940. But the aircraft industry was achieving miracles under the dynamic new Minister of Aircraft Production, Lord Beaverbrook. Whereas in February the industry had fallen 282 short of its planned production of 1,000 aircraft, in June it exceeded by 271 its planned total of 1,320 aircraft and delivered more than 1,600 in each of the two vital months that followed. Thus, by August 11th, Dowding had at his disposal 704 serviceable aircraft, of which 620 were Spitfires and Hurricanes. Equally important, the reserve of these types available for immediate supply to replace losses had risen from 36 to 289. On this still-slender force, and the skill and courage of a thousand pilots, rested the survival of Britain.

By itself, Fighter Command's force of front-line squadrons could not have won the battle that followed, but it was supported by a whole nation and Empire—and by the bloodied but unbeaten men in unfamiliar uniforms who had escaped from Poland, Czechoslovakia, France, Belgium, Holland and other countries, and had often suffered hardship and passed through incredible adventures before converging on Britain by sea and air to continue the fight. The extent of their contribution to victory is sometimes forgotten. Suffice it to say that the first of three wholly-Polish squadrons, No. 303, showed its burning hatred for the Germans by shooting down more enemy aircraft in the vital month of September 1940 than any other squadron in the Royal Air Force.

These men arrived fully-trained and ready for action. Nor were they the only pilots whose coming helped to ease the strain on those who wore R.A.F. blue. Soon after the outbreak of war, men (and later women, too) who were too old or not fit enough for combat flying formed an organisation known as Air Transport Auxiliary (A.T.A.) for the purpose of delivering light aircraft from factory to squadron and so releasing younger men for first-line duty. By the end of the war, these self-styled Ancient and Tattered Airmen had delivered no fewer than 308,567 aircraft, and it no longer caused a sensation when a five-foot-nothing girl or a middle-aged man with one arm stepped from a fighter—even a jet-fighter—or a four-engined bomber that had been delivered with a flourish at a front-line aerodrome.

It was, however, the raid reporting and fighter control system that, more than anything else, conserved the strength of Fighter Command in the Summer of 1940. By locating and tracking incoming attacks, it avoided the need for standing patrols that would have tired our pilots, used up our fuel reserves, and reduced the number of aircraft available to counter any particular threat. To achieve this, it used both the invisible eyes of radar and the keen human eyesight of the uniformed civilian members of the (later Royal) Observer Corps who stood in open wooden shelters atop hills and buildings, in all weathers, following and reporting by telephone every movement of every aeroplane by day and night.

Technically, the German *Freya* radar that had picked up the R.A.F.'s early bombing raids on Wilhelmshaven was comparable in quality with its British counterpart. It was in processing the data provided by radar and the Observer Corps, and passing it on to fighter pilots in their cockpits, that the British had a tremendous lead. This resulted from the Germans' belief that they had nothing to fear from allied bombers, with the result that most of their effort was put into offensive devices like radio beams to guide their own bombers to a target.

The R.A.F. did have a clear lead in airborne radar, small enough to be fitted in fighter and maritime patrol aircraft to help them to track down enemy aircraft and ships respectively, at night and in bad weather. As we have already seen, the anti-shipping (A.S.V.) type was first fitted to Hudson aircraft early in 1940. First with airborne interception (A.I.) radar were Blenheim Mk I fighters, which achieved their first success in a night action on July 22nd, 1940.

However, it was fortuitous that demands on Fighter Command's night flying force were not great at this period. The A.I. Mk.III radar fitted to the Blenheims extended the pilot's range of vision to around five miles, but its effectiveness disappeared when the distance between stalker and target closed to 800 ft., after which the pilot had to use his eyes. Development had been slowed by the priority given to setting up the Home Chain ground stations, and the Battle of Britain confirmed the soundness of this decision.

Not all of the United Kingdom's active defences were airborne. Anti-Aircraft Command had only 2,000 of the 8,000 guns it needed but they were skilfully deployed, with one quarter of the heavy guns protecting aircraft factories. Searchlights and barrage balloons were positioned with equal care and some key factories were given the added protection of a P.A.C. (Parachute and Cable) installation. Typical of many 'Heath Robinson' devices tested, and occasionally adopted, under wartime stress, P.A.C. consisted of a system of rockets which were fired electrically in the path of approaching enemy aircraft. They were intended to carry to a height of about 600 ft. light steel cables which were then lowered by parachute to enmesh any aircraft unfortunate enough to fly into them. Had the *Luftwaffe* attacked inland targets at low altitude in 1940, they might have proved a great asset.

The date fixed by Hitler for the start of his *Adlerangriff* was August 10th, 1940. The softening-up process began more than two months earlier, on the night of June 5/6th, when some 30 enemy bombers crossed the east coast to attack airfields and other targets. A similar effort was mounted on the following night, after which there was a ten-day pause while France was eliminated. The offensive was then resumed by up to 60 or 70 bombers every night. They achieved a certain nuisance value and gained operational experience, at the cost of one or two aircraft from each main force.

More significant were the German daylight attacks on convoys of merchant ships passing through the English Channel. Here, the *Luftwaffe* had the odds very much in its favour. With only a short distance to fly from its newly-won bases in France, it could pounce on a lightly escorted convoy and be on the way home before radar-alerted R.A.F. reinforcements arrived on the scene. Nonetheless, the heavily-outnumbered Spitfires and Hurricanes defended their charges with a skill and courage which the *Luftwaffe* would have done well to note.

During the month preceding August 10th, they shot from the skies a total of 227 enemy aircraft, for the loss of 96 R.A.F. machines. Lessons were learned on both sides. The Germans found to their cost that the Ju 87 dive-bomber, which had proved so effective against demoralised armies and civilians on the Continent, was a sitting duck for the pilots of Britain's eight-gun fighters. The R.A.F. learned the value of an efficient air/sea rescue service, to retrieve from the waters around these islands men who might live to fight again even though their aircraft had been destroyed.

The *Luftwaffe* already had such a service, using Heinkel He 59 floatplanes to pick up ditched aircrew. To make this task easier, even the pilots of Bf 109 single-seat fighters were provided with an inflatable dinghy, at a time when Hurricane and Spitfire pilots had to rely on their 'Mae West' life-jackets to keep them afloat.

Britain's first organised air/sea rescue units were equipped with R.A.F. high-speed launches, working in conjunction with borrowed Lysander search 'planes.   R.A.F. aircrew were supplied with fluorescine dye to stain the sea a bright green around them—another idea copied from the enemy.

These pioneer air/sea rescue units were to prove their worth over and over again when the battle began in earnest. So were improvements made to our fighters by the early Summer of 1940, such as an increase in the armour plate protecting the pilot and fuel tanks, introduction of self-sealing covering over fuel tanks to reduce the risk of fire from escaping petrol in combat or crash-landing, and the substitution of three-blade metal variable-pitch propellers for the old wooden fixed-pitch two-bladers, giving improvements in both speed and rate-of-climb.

Fighter Command had no illusions about the quality of the Bf 109 that was to be its main single-seat adversary. In May, the French had passed on, for testing by pilots of the Aircraft and Armament Experimental Establishment at Boscombe Down and Royal Aircraft Establishment at Farnborough one of two Bf 109Es which had been restored to an airworthy condition after forced landing in their territory.

Mock combats between the Bf 109 and R.A.F. fighters showed that its top speed (354 m.p.h. at 12,000 ft.) was little less than that of the Spitfire Mk.I (365 m.p.h. at 19,000 ft.) and superior to that of the Hurricane Mk.I (324 m.p.h. at 16,000 ft.). Although less manoeuvrable than a Spitfire, it had a better rate of climb and, with its fuel-injection engine, could escape from a difficult situation by snapping down into a dive. If the pilot of a British fighter tried to follow by pushing his stick forward suddenly, the resulting negative 'g' cut off the fuel supply to the carburettor of its Merlin engine which spluttered to a stop.

A similar assessment of the twin-engined Bf 110 became possible when, on July 10th, an aircraft of this type was brought down by a Spitfire, in Dorset, and was captured before its crew could set it on fire.

Such know-how was of tremendous value to the pilots of Fighter Command. Nor did they fear any longer the possibility of being out-gunned by the two or three longer-ranging 20-mm. cannon which supplemented the Bf 109's two machine-guns. Experience had shown that combats were usually fought at such close range that the point of convergence of their own eight machine-guns was reduced from the original 450 yards to 250 yards ahead of their aircraft.

Nobody doubted that Hitler would use against Britain every weapon in his armoury. Bomber Command tried to lessen the inevitable blow by attacking Germany's aircraft factories by night and airfields in occupied Europe by day; but with more than 400 such airfields available to the *Luftwaffe*, it was a hopeless task. In any case, attention had to be switched to the Channel ports when P.R.U. Spitfires and Hudsons discovered growing concentrations of barges that were clearly intended to carry the German army across the narrow seas.

It was almost a relief when, on August 8th, after two months of suspense, it seemed that the battle had begun at last. Again and again, the *Luftwaffe* struck at convoys off Dover and the Isle of Wight, losing 28 aircraft in the process, against 20 R.A.F. fighters. Unknown to anyone on this side of the Channel, the day appointed for the *Adlerangriff* passed without anything of particular note happening, because of adverse weather. Things hotted up on the 11th, when the *Luftwaffe* directed its attacks on Dover and Portland and on two convoys in the Channel. Destruction of 35 of the raiders was achieved only at the cost of 32 aircraft of Fighter Command. This was a ratio that had to be improved upon if the R.A.F. and Britain were to survive. It *was* improved when the full force of the *Luftwaffe* was unleashed against Britain's airfields and radar stations, as well as her Channel convoys, on the 12th.

As expected, No. 11 Group, commanded by Air Vice-Marshal K. R. Park from a headquarters at Uxbridge, had to take the full shock of the initial assault. Its thirteen squadrons of Hurricanes, six squadrons of Spitfires and two squadrons of Blenheims were dispersed throughout south-eastern England, inside an arc extending from Martlesham and Debden in the north to Tangmere in the south. Their task was made more difficult by the fact that the *Luftwaffe* struck at targets on or near the coast, giving minimum time for interception.

Radar plots left little doubt of the huge size of the aerial armadas approaching our coasts and the hearts of some of the Waafs in sector operations rooms must have missed a beat as they pushed markers representing hundreds of enemy aircraft across their maps, towards fighter stations and radar sites.

On the airfields of 11 Group, klaxons sounded and pilots at readiness grabbed their helmets and dashed towards the waiting

Hurricanes and Spitfires. With a skill born of endless practice, mechanics helped them on with their parachutes, and within seconds of the order to 'scramble', the fighters were airborne, their under-carriages tucking away into their wings as they climbed towards the known position of the enemy.

Whatever their pilots had been warned to expect by radio messages crackling through their earphones, the first sight of a *Luftwaffe* strike force must have been daunting. The daily pattern was always the same—many hundreds of aircraft, allocated to five or six major operations, despatched in such a way that a raid on one area would coincide with, or follow closely upon, attacks on another area many miles away.

Even Ju 87 dive-bombers were used in this opening phase of the battle, as the closeness of the targets to bases in France enabled the Germans to provide a strong fighter escort, despite the limited range of the Bf 109.

The tactics planned by Dowding and Park were for the Hurricanes to intercept the enemy bombers while the Spitfires tackled the higher-flying fighter escort. This made sense. At their rated altitude of around 15,000 feet the Hurricanes were a match for any *Luftwaffe* aircraft of that period, and the attacking bombers seldom flew above 17,000 feet. The engines of the Spitfires, on the other hand, were rated for optimum performance at 18,000 feet.

In practice, these tactics could not always be followed. In so hectic a battle, it was not easy to direct a balanced force of the two types of British fighter against each raid so that they arrived more or less simultaneously. If the 'Spits' were late, the Hurricane pilots had to fight off Bf 109s which dived on them from a much greater height and so had an initial advantage. And nobody had foreseen that some of the fighting would take place well above 20,000 feet, where the Bf 109 could out-perform even the Spitfire Mk.I.

The ideal proved to be for Fighter Command to engage the escorting Bf 109s at the earliest possible moment, so that the enemy pilots were forced to use up their fuel in combat and then return to base, leaving the bombers to their fate.

As at the time of the Dunkirk evacuation, it seemed that providence was on the side of those that fought against the crooked cross emblem of Nazi Germany. It was the kind of Summer that Englishmen remember as being typical of their youthful years but which seldom seems to occur now. Day after day the sun shone in a blue sky, with few clouds to afford protective cover for the Dorniers and Heinkels.

While the farmers of Southern England watched a fine harvest growing in their fields, curving white vapour trails high above showed where Fighter Command was reaping a grimmer harvest. From amid the corn sheaves, men from the wreckers' yards were soon busy gathering the corpses of *Luftflotten* 2, 3 and 5, so that experts could inspect the aircraft for clues to German technological progress, after which anything worth salvaging was removed.

Only a thousand pilots could fight the battle directly, but on the ground a whole nation worked with them and prayed for them. Production of aircraft to replace those that were lost ensured that Fighter Command was never reduced to a reserve of half-a-dozen Spitfires and Hurricanes, as has been implied on occasion, despite heavy raids on production centres. Housewives willingly handed over their precious aluminium pots and pans in the belief that these simple offerings could be transformed into Spitfires overnight.

Boys too young for the Services, and World War I veterans too old, queued to join the new Local Defence Volunteer force—soon renamed the Home Guard—and pledged themselves to answer Churchill's call to fight on the beaches, in the fields, on the landing grounds or anywhere that the enemy tried to set foot in Britain. Had their courage been tested, they would not have failed; but, fortunately, they were never to pit their vintage guns, home-made bombs—and even pikes—against the weight of the German army.

One vitally important facet of the air force's battle was that, as it was fought over Britain, enemy aircrew could escape from vanquished aircraft only to captivity in a prisoner-of-war camp. R.A.F. pilots baled out to fight again—sometimes within hours of clambering from a blazing or bullet-ridden aircraft. Only thus could Dowding lose 915 aircraft and still retain sufficient pilots to fly their replacements at a time when the training organisation was producing only six new pilots each day—and these, of course, lacking the experience and skill of the old hands.

In mid-August 1940, nobody could be sure that the sum of experience, courage, sound leadership, good aeroplanes, an efficient raid reporting organisation and other, less tangible, factors would be sufficient. The British people felt rather like King Canute, waiting for the tide to come in and with little save a bold voice to turn it back. It was as well they could not hear the voices of German soldiers on the other side of the narrow seas, chanting 'We March against England' as their boots thundered over the cobble-stones towards the Channel ports. In their turn, the soldiers wished they could not hear the little Dutch boys, marching cheekily beside them and chanting: 'Splash, splash, splash' to remind them of the sea and the Royal Navy.

They, too, need not have worried . . .

Despite the weight of the *Luftwaffe's* onslaught on August 12th, it had not greatly reduced Fighter Command's strength. One airfield, at Manston, had been put out of action; those at Hawkinge and Lympne had received such heavy poundings that great skill was needed to take off and land on the narrow strips of grass that remained clear of craters. Five of the precious warning radar stations had been hit and must have looked to the Germans as if they would play no further part in the battle. In fact, four of them were operational next day and only that on the Isle of Wight was destroyed.

Thus, while the *Luftwaffe* was startled to discover that all its major raids had been intercepted and 36 of its aircraft lost (against 22 R.A.F. machines), its crews returned fully confident that the first nail had been driven into the R.A.F.'s coffin. Even worse miscalculations were to follow.

August 13th must have seemed to the Germans one of the rare days during the Battle of Britain when everything would be in their favour from the start. It was cloudy; so, believing they had knocked out much of the radar warning system, the bomber crews expected to approach their targets undetected and unseen. The plan this day was to probe the defences all the way from Southampton to Southend, as it seemed impossible that an already-weakened fighter force could protect all of south-east England and the *Luftwaffe* wanted to find the weak spots.

There weren't any. Only the city of Southampton and the Coastal Command stations of Detling and Eastchurch were seriously damaged. Those crews who broke through the defences to reach seven Fighter Command airfields dropped a few bombs, at high cost. Forty-seven German aircraft failed to return to their bases, against the loss of 13 R.A.F. machines.

Throughout the Battle of Britain—indeed, throughout the war—claims by both sides of the number of enemy aircraft destroyed in daylight air combat were found to be exaggerated when it became possible to check the actual losses from official records after the war. This is understandable.

Often, aircraft that were destroyed were under simultaneous fire from two opposing aircraft, or from an aircraft and anti-aircraft guns, and R.A.F. pilots were forbidden to follow down a suspected victim simply to confirm that it had crashed. In addition, the battles of August and September 1940 were so hectic and numerous that interrogation of pilots in the brief periods between landing and take-off was difficult. Pilots often landed away from their home base and, with airfields as the prime target of the *Luftwaffe*, communications were difficult.

The resulting inflated claims had very different effects on the two sides engaged in the battle—both favourable to the R.A.F. Whilst under no delusion that the *Luftwaffe* would be beaten quickly, the pilots of Fighter Command were elated by their successes and, of course, the British public derived fresh heart and inspiration from the daily 'score-sheets'.

In Germany, General Stapf reminded General Halder of his July 11th prediction that it would take between a fortnight and a month to smash the R.A.F. Now, in only five days, since August 8th, he felt able to report that eight British air bases had been destroyed and that the R.A.F. was losing three aircraft for every *Luftwaffe* machine lost—the ratio for fighter losses being five to one.

Halder may have believed this, but Reichsmarschall Goering, the old fighter pilot, seems to have been less convinced. Gathering air force commanders together at his Prussian home on August 15th he ordered that operations should be directed exclusively against the Royal Air Force and the aircraft factories supplying its aircraft. However tempting other targets might seem, particularly large naval vessels, they were to be ignored. Furthermore, to minimise the loss of experienced aircrew, no aircraft operating over the U.K. was to contain more than one officer.

This was sound advice, but Goering made one fatal error. Realising, after the experience of August 12/13th, that it was less easy to knock out radar stations than had been anticipated, he said that there seemed to be little point in repeating attacks on them. His observation was interpreted as an order and little more was done to prevent every marauding *Luftwaffe* fighter and bomber from being pin-pointed and tracked by radar and the Observer Corps.

The daylight attacks of August 13th had been followed by the first of a series of night raids on aircraft factories. Up to that time the *Luftwaffe* had attempted little but mine-laying under cover of darkness. It was, therefore, to the credit of *Kampfgruppe* 100 that the crews of its He 111s managed to hit the Spitfire factory at Castle Bromwich with seven bombs at the first attempt.

Fortunately for Britain, this did not reflect the true level of efficiency of Germany's limited night bomber force. During the next ten nights, eight attacks aimed at the Bristol factory at Filton produced damage on only two occasions. In nine operations directed against the Gloster, Rolls-Royce and Westland plants, the bombs landed within five miles of the target only twice.

On the 14th, the most significant incident was an attack on Manston by nine Bf 110s, which were taking over the tasks performed earlier by Ju 87s. The latter were clearly unable to live in the same sky as Fighter Command and it did not take long to convince the Germans that the Bf 110s were equally vulnerable, after which they were withdrawn from the Channel coast.

Although nobody in Britain could know it at the time, the following day, August 15th, decided the outcome of the daylight battles over the United Kingdom. For the first time, weather conditions were suitable for the *Luftwaffe* to implement its original plan of flinging the full might of three *Luftflotten* into the attack.

While *Luftflotte* 2 was making the first of five major raids on south-east England, each mounted by 70 to 150 aircraft, and *Luftflotte* 3 prepared to launch between 200 and 300 aircraft in the south, General Stumpff despatched two *Luftflotte* 5 armadas from bases in Norway and Denmark.

The first was picked up by radar when it was still nearly 100 miles from the British coast. As the signals appeared to indicate about 30 enemy aircraft, No. 72 Squadron from Acklington had no hesitation in making the first interception unaided. Nor did the Spitfire pilots change their mind when they discovered that, in fact, there were about 100 He 111s, escorted by 70 Bf 110s. Tearing into the huge formations, they so surprised and shattered the German aircrews that the force was split in two.

No. 79 (Spitfire) Squadron, also from Acklington, next pounced on one of the resulting, still-large formations, doing such deadly execution that the Bf 110s, short of fuel, turned tail and fled for home as soon as they reached the coastline.

Now it was the turn of Nos. 41, 605 and 607 Squadrons, whose 'Spits' and 'Hurris' tore into the unescorted bombers with such fury that not a single military objective suffered any damage.

Luftflotte 5's second raid fared little better. Its 50 Ju 88s found four Fighter Command squadrons waiting for them as they headed for Scarborough. On the credit side, they bombed an ammunition dump near Bridlington, probably by accident, and heavily damaged the aerodrome at Driffield, where ten aircraft were destroyed on the ground. On the other side of the balance sheet, Stumpff's air fleet had paid so heavily for its modest successes that it did not again put in a daylight appearance over north-eastern Britain during the remaining weeks of the battle. In one day, it had lost an eighth of its bombers and a fifth of its long-range fighters.

As the American air forces were to learn to their dismay in later years, a bomber force had to expect such treatment if it ventured over hostile territory in daylight without an effective fighter escort.

In the south, the *Luftwaffe* achieved much more on this August day. Several airfields were hit and the aircraft industry suffered heavy blows. At Rochester, the Short and Pobjoy factories were put out of action for several weeks. At Croydon, the Rollason and Redwing factories were severely damaged. But No. 11 Group also distinguished itself. One raid was met by the record total of 150 Spitfires and Hurricanes, and the total of destruction on the ground was unbelievably small when one bears in mind that no fewer than 520 bombers and 1,270 fighters took part in the day's attacks.

That evening, the B.B.C. told its listeners at home and abroad—many with clandestine radios in occupied Europe—that 182 enemy aircraft had been destroyed, with another 53 probables. The true figure for the day was 76, against 34 R.A.F. aircraft—still bad enough for the Germans to refer to August 15th as *schwarzer Donnerstag* (black Thursday).

Day after day the battle went on. To the hard-pressed fighter pilots, controllers and ground crews, the *Luftwaffe* must have seemed like a 20th century counterpart of Hydra, the beast of Greek mythology which, every time Heracles lopped off one of its nine heads, grew two more.

On August 16th, a total of 1,720 aircraft droned across the Channel. It was some encouragement that more than 1,300 of them were fighters, but the weight of the attack was beginning to tell in several ways. At Brize Norton, 46 aircraft were destroyed in their hangars. Fortunately, it was not a fighter station, but three of the other seven airfields attacked that day were used by Fighter Command, and on the 18th every hangar but one at the important sector station of Kenley was destroyed.

In ten days, Fighter Command had shot down 367 enemy aircraft, against its own loss of 183 in combat and 30 on the ground. Splendid as this might appear on paper, in fact it was disastrous, for production of Spitfires and Hurricanes totalled little more than 100 a week and there were only 230 in reserve. In the same period, 154 pilots had been killed, posted as missing or severely wounded, and only 63 replacements had come from the training organisation.

Miraculously, heavy cloud prevented the *Luftwaffe* from making any major attacks between the 19th and the 23rd, giving the R.A.F. a much-needed breather. But when the onslaught was renewed, it took on a changed and more sinister form. Realising that the nerve centres of No. 11 Group were the seven sector stations of Tangmere, Debden, Kenley, Biggin Hill, Hornchurch, North Weald and Northolt—each of which directed by radio three squadrons to intercept incoming attacks—the *Luftwaffe* went all out to remove these key bases.

Kenley had been hard hit on the 18th. It was North Weald's turn on the 24th, with lesser damage at Hornchurch. On the 26th bombs fell at Debden, but determined attacks on Hornchurch and North Weald were beaten off. Four days later, Biggin Hill suffered its first heavy pounding. On the 31st, Debden was bombed, but it was Hornchurch and Biggin that bore the brunt of the last big raid of the day.

By the first day of September, the airfield at Manston was out of action and the sector stations of Kenley and Biggin Hill were groggy. On that day, the enemy went all out for the kill at Biggin and by evening hardly a building remained standing or safe for use: yet the station remained operational. The 'heroes' were the girls of the W.A.A.F., like telephonists Sgt. Helen Turner and Cpl. Elspeth Henderson who stayed at their post even after the block in which they were working had suffered a direct hit.

Such spirit was unbeatable. For six more days the sector stations were subjected to constant attack, but still the Hurricanes and Spitfires were there to meet, and usually break up, every raid. From August 24th until September 6th, an average of almost 1,000 aircraft a day were hurled against targets in Britain; on the 30th and 31st, the attacks numbered over 1,600 each day. By now, bombers seldom made up more than one quarter of each formation, but there was little reason for optimism, for the number of Hurricanes and Spitfires available for immediate issue to replace losses had fallen to 125. Furthermore, attacks on the Vickers and Hawker factories at Weybridge on September 4th and 6th respectively made it appear likely that the aircraft industry was about to receive the same priority treatment as sector airfields.

Overnight, through the intervention of a miracle that came to be known as 'Hitler's intuition', the whole situation changed.

Stung by a series of Bomber Command night raids on Berlin, which were of propaganda value rather than militarily worthwhile, the *Führer* decided to direct the full might of the *Luftwaffe* against

London.   The invasion of Britain had again been deferred from
September 15th to the 21st.   Even at this late stage, it might prove
unnecessary if London could be subjected to the same measure of
devastation as Rotterdam had suffered in the Spring.

August 15th had seen an end to German hopes of swamping
Britain's air defences by simultaneous attacks with three *Luftflotten*.
This new decision by Hitler destroyed any remaining possibility
that the *Luftwaffe* might win the Battle of Britain.   Unlike Rotterdam,
London was far from being an open city; and Fighter Command,
its radar system intact and its sector airfields no longer under
relentless hammering from enemy bombers, could face up to the
new situation with the confidence gained in nearly a month of daily
victories against the air force that had thought itself invincible.

The first day of the new offensive must have persuaded Hitler
that he was right again.   Huge formations of bombers, heavily
escorted by fighters, smashed a way past the defences and attacked
the Arsenal and other targets at Woolwich, Thameshaven and the
docks at West Ham.   Twenty-one R.A.F. squadrons engaged the
attackers, but most of the 40 enemy aircraft destroyed were fighters
and 21 Spitfires and Hurricanes were lost.

It seemed that the whole river was ablaze from Thameshaven
eastward, and the 250 bombers that came over London in a continuous stream from 8 o'clock in the evening until 4 a.m. next morning
had no difficulty in finding their targets and adding to the inferno
with 300 tons of high-explosive and 13,000 incendiary bombs.   Only
one bomber was shot down that night.

Encouraged by this early success, the Germans decided to continue
making heavy night raids on London, when darkness would reduce
their losses to negligible proportions, and to use only small bomber
formations by daylight, heavily escorted by fighters which could
complete the elimination of Fighter Command *en route* to and from
London.

They were quickly disillusioned.   The 100 bombers which set out
in daylight to keep the fires burning in London's dockland on
September 8th failed to get near the target.   Next day, an even
larger force was repelled by British fighter squadrons that were
clearly not down to their last 100 aircraft, as Goering had believed.
Then the weather lent a hand once more, and only one sizeable
raid was possible in the next five days, although odd aircraft managed
to lob their bombs onto the Admiralty, the War Office and
Buckingham Palace.   The people of London, who were withstanding

the day and night assault far more cheerfully and bravely than anyone could have expected, felt both angry and inspired by the fact that their King and Queen (who, like them, refused to leave London) were so clearly sharing their dangers and loss.

The 15th was another big day, with more than 1,000 aircraft despatched against London. A record total of 185 enemy machines was claimed as destroyed, and this date is still remembered in Britain as the climax of the battle although, in fact, the Germans lost only 56 aircraft, against 26 R.A.F. machines. Damage to London was slight and the officer charged with keeping the War Diary at German War Headquarters had to record: 'The enemy air force is still by no means defeated; on the contrary it shows increasing activity. The weather situation as a whole does not permit us to expect a period of calm . . . The Führer therefore decides to postpone Sea Lion indefinitely.'

Although nobody in Britain could yet appreciate it, the battle had been won and the United Kingdom was never again to come so near to invasion. For the rest of the month, the *Luftwaffe* continued its attempts to destroy aircraft factories and to smash its way through to London; but it achieved little and the final straw came on September 30th when three fruitless raids cost 47 aircraft against 20 Spitfires and Hurricanes lost in combat. From that time on, only the Messerschmitts attempted to penetrate Britain's defences in any numbers by day, while the bombers sought the cover of darkness for their continued 'blitz' on London.

It was a tremendous victory for the Royal Air Force—psychologically as well as militarily. With the *Luftwaffe* driven from the daylight skies over Britain, it was inconceivable that the war could now be lost, however long and however costly the struggle might be. As always, Winston Churchill spoke for the whole British people when he commented, in the House of Commons: 'Never in the field of human conflict was so much owed by so many to so few.'

What kind of men were these 'few' who saved Britain? Many were the carefree long-haired undergraduates of the University Air Squadrons of the 'thirties; others were Poles, with a fierce hatred for the *Luftwaffe*. There was the legless Bader, returning to fighter operations after a pre-war crash to become a great leader and vanquisher of more than 20 enemy aircraft. And there was J. B. Nicolson of No. 249 Squadron, who delayed jumping by parachute from his blazing Hurricane until he had shot down a Bf 110 which suddenly came into his sights—and thereby earned the only Victoria Cross awarded in the Battle of Britain.

These men, and their brothers at arms, were the last of the colourful 'knights in shining armour' who set off to engage the enemy in single-handed combat. A different breed was needed now for the grim, seemingly unending war of attrition that would one day bring Germany to its knees.

Chapter Three

Parry and Thrust Europe: October 1940 - September 1941

The bomb had fallen in Peckham. It was a very big one—probably a land-mine . . . When my car was recognised the people came running from all quarters . . . They crowded round us, cheering and manifesting every sign of lively affection . . . When we got back into the car a harsher mood swept over this haggard crowd. 'Give it 'em back', they cried . . . I undertook forthwith to see that their wishes were carried out; and this promise was certainly kept.

Winston Churchill. The Second World War, Vol. Two

FIGHTER COMMAND IS honoured justly for winning the battle in the Summer skies of Britain in 1940; but every R.A.F. Command played its part in defeating Hitler's plans to invade the United Kingdom.

As early as May 16th, 1940, Training Command Operational Order No. 1 outlined a scheme for fitting racks for 20-lb. bombs on the Tiger Moth biplanes and Harvards based at Flying Training Schools, so that they could be used to attack incoming enemy invasion barges. This order was superseded by another, under which the Spitfires and Hurricanes allocated to Operational Training Units would form into squadrons to supplement the front-line fighter force on receipt of the code-word 'Saracen', signifying invasion.

The O.T.U.'s were numbered from 51 upward and, on becoming squadrons, would have added 500 to their unit designation. Later, however, under Operation Banquet, each was expected to produce *two* squadrons and No. 58 O.T.U. at Grangemouth, for example, would have formed Nos. 558 and 563 Squadrons with its Hurricanes and flown them from Turnhouse. In the event, 'Saracen' was never transmitted and the O.T.U.'s continued their vital task of feeding new pilots to the combat squadrons.

The achievements of Bomber Command in those Summer months are remembered only a little better; yet they were of tremendous significance, both operationally and psychologically.

Up to mid-1940, the war had brought only frustration to this Command. Early losses had compelled it to switch its 'heavies' from daylight to night operations. Much of its effort had been devoted to the futile task of showering propaganda leaflets on an enemy whose strength and confidence were unlikely to be affected by paper bombs after conquering half of Europe in a few weeks. Even its well-organised plan to attack targets in Italy, after that country's belated entry into the war, had collapsed into a fiasco.

Anticipating that Mussolini would emerge as an ally of Germany in time to share the spoils of an imminent French defeat, the Supreme War Cabinet had despatched No. 71 Wing Headquarters to the Marseilles area in early June, to prepare two airfields for use by R.A.F. Wellingtons. The idea was that the bombers would land at these bases to refuel, *en route* from the U.K. to the industrial centres of Northern Italy, while longer-range Whitleys refuelled in the Channel Islands.

Uninspiringly code-named 'Haddock', the operation was viewed with complete lack of enthusiasm by the French, who believed that every effort should be directed against the main enemy in the north and that R.A.F. raids on Italy would simply provoke retaliation against Marseilles, Lyons and Paris. The controversy reached its peak during the afternoon and evening of June 11th, when Wellingtons of No. 99 Squadron landed at Salon airfield to open the offensive.

The commander of a nearby French bomber group said that the operation must be cancelled. The Air Ministry ordered the attack to continue. General Vuillemin, French Chief of Air Staff, telephoned the British Air Forces in France H.Q. and demanded that Air Marshal Barratt should forbid take-off. Barratt contacted the Air Ministry, who referred him to the Prime Minister . . . but Churchill was on his way to France. After several hours of heated order and counter-order, at successively higher level, the Wellingtons began taxying out on to the airfield. Simultaneously, French lorries drove out and took up a pre-arranged formation that made take-off and landing impossible.

Nor did the 36 Whitleys of Nos. 10, 51, 58, 77 and 102 Squadrons achieve much more. After refuelling in the Channel Islands, they battled through heavy storms and severe icing and only 13 of them reached Turin and Genoa. Similar conditions were met by the

Wellingtons of 99 and 149 Squadrons which were permitted to fly from Salon on the 15th, and only one aircraft dropped its bombs on Genoa. On the 16th, four of a force of nine Wellingtons failed to find their target. Twenty-four hours later, France asked for an armistice and the R.A.F. lost all the forward bases which had been regarded for two decades as a key factor in Bomber Command's plans for attacking German targets in the event of war.

To a degree this was irrelevant. Many primary targets were now not in Germany but on or near the Channel coast, all too close to bomber bases in the U.K. Day after day, *Luftwaffe* airfields in occupied territory were attacked in an effort to ease the pressure on Fighter Command. Each day, too, the Spitfires and Hudsons of Cotton's Photographic Reconnaissance Unit flew along the full length of the enemy coastline, from the Texel to Cherbourg, seeking out and photographing the mounting fleet of invasion craft.

By September 6th, there were 205 barges at Ostend alone. The number at Flushing increased by 120 in a week; in three days the total at Dunkirk and Calais went up by 87. These ominous preparations and the sudden switch in the *Luftwaffe's* main attacks, from fighter stations to London, on September 7th led to the issue of Alert No. 1—'Invasion imminent and probable within twelve hours.'

At this crucial moment, the whole of Bomber Command was unleashed against the enemy-held ports, pounding ships and barges, assembled troops and stores, roads and railways leading to the ports, and gun emplacements, by day and night. The invasion fleet continued to multiply, until there were more than 1,000 barges in harbour and another 600 up-river at Antwerp on September 18th. But by then Fighter Command over Southern England and Bomber Command over the invasion coastline had persuaded Hitler to call off Operation Sea Lion.

Twelve per cent of his barges had been wrecked in a fortnight—80 of them in a single raid on Ostend on the 13th—and it would clearly be suicidal to commit the remainder to a cross-Channel venture through seas still guarded by the Royal Navy and an air force that refused to be beaten. On September 23rd, P.R.U. Spitfires reported that at least a third of the one-time invasion force had already dispersed.

Instead of the soldiers of the *Wehrmacht*, Britain—and London in particular—now had to contend with the 'blitz'. Between September 7th and November 13th, more than 12,000 night sorties were flown over the U.K. London received over 13,000 tons of high explosive and nearly one million incendiary bombs in a non-stop nightly offensive such as no other city has ever had to endure for so long a period. Fortunately, London is a big place, peopled by men, women and children who possess a traditional blend of fortitude and humour. Thirteen thousand of them died in September and October alone, with another 20,000 injured; but cruel as they were, such statistics revealed only how little the *Luftwaffe* was achieving.

One civilian killed for each ton of bombs dropped was a return that would never win the war. Docks, railways and other important targets had suffered their share of destruction, but life went on. Buses took commuters around shattered stations, ships continued to load and unload, and Londoners who slept safely in underground railway stations by night popped out of their 'rabbit holes' next morning, saddened by the latest signs of damage but no less determined to see it through.

In retrospect, it is easy to dismiss London's ordeal with the comment that, later in the war, some cities in Germany and Japan suffered higher casualties and proportionally greater destruction in a single raid than London incurred between September 7th and November 13th, 1940. However, even ancient Chinese torturers knew that it is the continued dripping of tiny water droplets on the head of a victim that induces moral breakdown rather than a sudden deluge. There was nothing wrong with the psychology of sending 150 to 300 bombers over London every night, spreading their attack over as many hours as possible. The objective was, simply, too vast and the weapons—averaging little more than a ton of bombs per aircraft—too small.

Goering never believed that the 'blitz' would subdue London. He pleaded with Hitler to allow the bombers to attack smaller, militarily-significant targets, and at last he got his way.

On the night of November 14/15th, a total of 437 enemy aircraft took off in three great streams converging on Coventry. At their head, as pathfinders, were the He 111's of *K.Gr.*100, whose pilots specialised in precision attacks against small targets by night.

Dr. R. V. Jones and his colleagues in Scientific Intelligence had already learned to jam the primitive *Knickebein* radio navigation aid which the *Luftwaffe* had hoped to use to find its targets. This time *K.Gr.*100 used the more complicated *X-Gerät* system, which involved flying along a fine radio beam, centred in a coarse beam, until a succession of intersecting beams signalled distance-to-target. It worked well. *K.Gr.*100 showered the first incendiaries on Coventry at 8.15 p.m. For nearly ten hours, the main force then released over the blazing city a total of 394 tons of high-explosive, 56 tons of incendiary bombs and 127 parachute mines.

To the British public as a whole, Coventry had been little more than a cathedral city. Now the cathedral was gone, 380 people had been killed and the name of Coventry was regarded as being synonymous with Rotterdam as a symbol of German beastliness in attacking civilian targets. This was not entirely justified. Most *Luftwaffe* crews had been allocated specific targets of military importance and the buildings hit included twelve aircraft factories and nine other important industrial plants. Output of aircraft in the U.K. slumped briefly by 20 per cent—for the loss of but one enemy bomber.

Coventry set the pattern for this second phase of the 'blitz', which lasted until the end of February 1941. London was not left in peace, as eight of the 31 major raids mounted in this period were directed against the capital. Fourteen of the others were concentrated against other ports and nine on inland centres of industry. Southampton, Birmingham, Liverpool, Bristol, Plymouth, Manchester, Sheffield, Cardiff, Portsmouth and Avonmouth all felt the weight of *Luftwaffe* attack, often with two or three raids in quick succession. Fortunately, the weather took a hand in the first weeks of the new year, cutting the number of enemy sorties from 6,000 in November 1940 to only 1,200 in February 1941.

In this, it was more effective than Britain's defences. A mere 81 aircraft—less than one per cent of the forces engaged—were claimed as destroyed during the 'blitz' on London, and only eight of these were shot down by fighters. The actual total was found to be higher after the war, but still insignificant. During the second phase, up to the end of February, the percentage dropped further, with 75 aircraft destroyed in more than 12,000 sorties. The only encouraging feature was that one-third of the successes were credited to fighters.

Nobody doubted that the effectiveness of the R.A.F.'s night fighter force was about to be increased beyond measure. Newly-introduced Beaufighters, with a top speed of 330 m.p.h., unprecedented armament of four 20-mm. cannon and six machine-guns, and A.I.Mk.IV radar, were already accounting for half the kills claimed by fighter squadrons at night. The secret of their success was that they were directed to their targets by ground controllers, who could see both the enemy bomber and intercepting fighter on the screen of their G.C.I. (ground control of interception) radar.

Once again, British science and invention were paying rich dividends. Some guns were now radar directed, and they were supplemented by rocket batteries and a variety of experimental devices, some more practical than others.

One of the less successful was 'Mutton', which involved dropping in the path of enemy bombers 2,000 ft. lengths of piano wire, each with a parachute at one end and a bomb at the other. The chance of an aircraft tangling with such a trap in the immensity of airspace over the U.K. was clearly minute; the only pilots really endangered by 'Mutton' were those at the Royal Aircraft Establishment who flew deliberately into unarmed versions in an effort to develop the weapon's potential.

The real success stories could not be told at the time, because of the need for strict secrecy, and are little better known today. The undercover 'battle' of electronic countermeasures was, perhaps, the most fascinating of all, and certainly one of the most vital.

Having discovered and dealt with *Knickebein*, Dr. Jones next concentrated on *X-Gerät*. Jamming devices known as 'Bromides' were issued to the specially-formed No. 80 Wing, commanded by Wing-Cdr. E. B. Addison. Within a few days of the Coventry raid, the pathfinder crews of *K.Gr.*100 made a far less satisfactory job of marking Birmingham; the main force became lost and scattered their bombs over a wide area. By mid-January 1941, every important target in Southern England was protected by a 'Bromide' jammer.

German scientists thought they had the answer in a more complicated radio aid known as *Y-Gerät*. But the R.A.F. monitoring system picked up *Y-Gerät* signals while the system was still at an early stage of development. By the time it became operational, Dr. Robert Cockburn of the Telecommunications Research Establishment already had the perfect answer in the form of his 'Domino' jammer.

With their radio navigation aids in a state of disorder, *Luftwaffe* crews became increasingly susceptible to decoys, and this was yet another highly-secret field in which Britain excelled. King of the decoys was Colonel (later Sir) John F. Turner, a retired Air Ministry Director of Works and Buildings, who set out enthusiastically to deceive and confuse the *Luftwaffe*. By June 1940, there were about 70 bogus airfields dispersed between the R.A.F.'s operational stations, some complete with full-scale wooden aeroplanes, most with flare-paths and other lights to attract marauding enemy bombers by night.

The dummy airfields were a brilliant success. So were Col. Turner's decoy fires, code-named 'Starfish', which were designed to light up in the path of a bomber force at just the right moment to look like markers dropped by enemy pathfinders. The first time 'Starfish' was used, on December 2nd, 1940, it collected 66 bombs intended for Bristol. The total weight that fell on Col. Turner's airfields and other decoys was astronomical. On April 17/18th alone, a 'Starfish' site at Hayling Island collected 170 high-explosive bombs, 32 parachute mines and 5,000 incendiary bombs. On May 9th, the German radio claimed that heavy damage had been inflicted on Derby and Nottingham during the previous night, notably at the Rolls-Royce works. In fact, a combination of 'Bromide' and 'Starfish' had limited casualties to two cows and a pair of chickens.

When the final phase of the 'blitz' began on February 19th, 1941, Britain was therefore much better prepared than had been the case a few months earlier. By the time it ended, on May 12th, London had been subjected to seven very heavy raids, Birmingham five, Coventry two and Nottingham one. But the remaining 46 were directed against ports.

Hitler had decided to attack Russia in June of that year, leaving Britain to be starved into submission by the U-boat offensive at sea and sustained air attacks on her ports and shipyards. Only the aircraft industry was to retain any priority so far as other targets were concerned.

Avonmouth, Belfast, Bristol, Clydeside, Hull, Merseyside, Newcastle, Plymouth, Portsmouth, Sunderland and Swansea all received attention from Goering's bombers. Some German pilots became skilled in sea-level skip-bombing attacks on ships at sea, and mine-laying in British waters was intensified. Yet the air offensive in the first five months of 1941 robbed the U.K. of only 70,000 tons of food and one-half of one per cent of its stocks of oil.

On the credit side, R.A.F. fighters claimed 22 enemy bombers destroyed in March, 48 in April and 96 in May—figures we now know to be at least 30 per cent below the actual German losses. Clearly the defences were beginning to become effective; but the enemy losses still represented only some $3\frac{1}{2}$ per cent of the attacking force and it was Hitler's obsession with eliminating Russia rather than mounting casualties that caused the enemy bomber fleets to start flying east instead of west.

What lessons could R.A.F. Bomber Command learn from all this? The answers were far from encouraging, as they suggested the need for heavy attacks by large forces, which it didn't have; the use of difficult-to-jam radio navigation aids, which it also lacked; and concentration on specific, particularly vulnerable types of target such as the aircraft industry, which was unlikely to be permitted in view of the Admiralty's insistance on massive R.A.F. support in the war at sea.

The Command's brief was clear enough. In early September, before the Battle of Britain had reached its climax, Winston Churchill had put before the War Cabinet a minute stating: 'The Navy can lose us the war, but only the Air Force can win it. Therefore our supreme effort must be to gain overwhelming mastery in the air. The fighters are our salvation, but the bombers alone provide the means of victory. We must, therefore, develop the power to carry an ever-increasing volume of explosives to Germany, so as to pulverize the entire industry and scientific structure on which the war effort and economic life of the enemy depend, while holding him at arm's length from our island. In no other way at present visible can we hope to overcome the immense military power of Germany.'

The Prime Minister's logic was unarguable, but the R.A.F.'s bombers were neither specifically designed nor equipped for the task now given them. They lacked the range to hit effectively places like Berlin, which was five times as far from British bomber bases as was London from *Luftwaffe* airfields. Thus, on September 23/24th, 1940, 84 of a total force of 119 Whitleys, Wellingtons and Hampdens succeeded in completing the long flight to the German capital, but in terms of military value it was a waste of effort.

At this time, R.A.F. night bomber crews were still allocated specific targets and often spent a half-hour or more cruising around trying to find them. They were seldom successful unless there was some specific landmark such as a river estuary or large lake; but equally they were not in any great danger. The enemy air defences were even less effective than those of the U.K. after dark—perhaps because Goering had given his personal promise that no British bombs would ever fall on Germany.

The early months of 1941 ought to have given the Reichsmarschall ominous warning of how unwise his words had been. Back in 1936, the British Air Staff had conceived specifications for a new generation of super-bombers, and these were now becoming operational.

First to see action, on the night of February 10/11th, 1941, were the Short Stirlings of No. 7 Squadron. Powered by four 1,595 h.p. Hercules radials, the Stirling had a maximum speed of 270 m.p.h., was armed with eight machine-guns in three turrets, and could fly 590 miles with 14,000 lb. of bombs or 2,010 miles with 3,500 lb.

Specification B.12/36, to which it was designed, had limited its wing span to that which could be accommodated in standard R.A.F. hangars. Coupled with a loaded weight of 31 tons, this necessitated a low aspect ratio wing and, as a result, the Stirling's service ceiling was only 17,000 ft. In addition, its stalky main undercarriage had a tendency to collapse, and its segmented bomb-bay could not take anything bigger than a 4,000-pounder. Nonetheless, its heavy armament enabled it to operate over France by day as well as night throughout 1941, initially without fighter escort and later as a replacement for Blenheims in escorted 'Circuses' which had the added purpose of making *Luftwaffe* fighters take off to do battle.

It was followed closely by the Avro Manchester, designed to Specification P.13/36 which called for the use of two 1,760 h.p. Rolls-Royce Vulture engines. Quite early in the development programme, it began to look as if this bomber would be under-powered and there were good reasons to fear that the engines might prove unreliable. Handley Page had already been instructed to revise their P.13/36 design, the Halifax, to take four Merlins instead of two Vultures; Avro wanted to do the same, but were refused permission to do so. Undeterred, they by-passed normal distribution channels to collect together sufficient raw materials for a prototype with four Merlins, and the result became, eventually, the Lancaster, finest of all the night bombers of World War II.

Meanwhile, the Manchester bore out Avro's fears. Seven squadrons persevered with it on operations for more than a year while Rolls tried to cure persistent engine failures; but the type was finally withdrawn from service in June 1942.

It was left to the Halifax to demonstrate fully the far-sightedness of the pre-war decision to order big bombers. It began operations, with No. 35 Squadron, on 11/12th March, 1941, and went on eventually to share with the Lancaster the task of maintaining the R.A.F.'s great night bomber offensive; but its crews suffered initially from the same frustrations as the rest of Bomber Command, summed up as follows by Air Marshal Sir Robert Saundby.*

'Throughout 1941, the Command struggled to carry out its task, with insufficient numbers and inadequate equipment. It was a year of frustrated effort and hope deferred. There had been no effective shift of priorities to the requirements of the air offensive. Indeed, our mounting losses at sea, and the painful inability of the Royal Navy to cope with the submarine menace, caused the Prime Minister,

---

* "Bomber Command 1939–42", an article in *Aircraft Seventy* (Ian Allan Ltd, 1969)

on March 6th, to give absolute priority to the Battle of the Atlantic. Additional squadrons of long-range aircraft for anti-submarine warfare could be found from only one source, and during 1941 no fewer than 17 squadrons were transferred to Coastal Command. They were supposed to be on loan, but none of them ever returned. In addition, a considerable number of aircraft with crews were transferred to the North African theatre.   As a result, Bomber Command ended a year of great effort with no increase in strength, and indeed weakened by casualties and its unsuccessful efforts to expand.'

Even worse, a careful assessment of raid reports, and photographs taken by the light of flash bombs at the moment of bomb release during 100 raids, showed that only one aircraft in three had made its attack within five miles of its designated target. Over the Ruhr, the average fell to one aircraft in ten. So much effort, so many lives had been expended for so very little. The road ahead was indeed long.

Chapter Four

Africa, Middle East and Mediterranean: June 1940 - May 1943

There is another reason why the Battle of Alamein will survive. It marked the turning of 'the Hinge of Fate'. It may almost be said, 'Before Alamein we never had a victory. After Alamein we never had a defeat.'

Winston Churchill. *The Second World War, Vol. Four*

BACK IN THE Summer of 1917, the pilots of a single flight of five Sopwith Triplanes of No. 10 (Naval) Squadron destroyed 87 German aircraft in three months over the Western Front. Their leader, Flt. Sub-Lt. Raymond Collishaw from Canada, went on to claim 60 victories in air combat—a total exceeded only by Mannock and Bishop in the British air forces.

When Italy entered the war, on June 10th, 1940, this same Ray Collishaw commanded No. 202 Group, the R.A.F. units in the Western Desert of Egypt. He sent his bombers into action against El Adem, Italy's main air base in Cyrenaica, at dawn on the following day. By the end of the month, 202 Group had established complete moral superiority over the more numerous enemy air forces. In daylight, its Blenheims attacked airfields, ports and any Italian troops unfortunate enough to be spotted by the eager aircrew. By night, the Bombay bomber-transports of No. 216 Squadron took over, with Tobruk as their primary target. Gladiators provided escort for the Blenheims and kept enemy raiders at bay. Lysanders of 208 Squadron watched every move by Italian troops in forward areas.

When the Royal Navy bombarded Bardia, on August 17th, the Gladiators shot down eight SM.79 bombers sent to attack the ships, without loss to themselves. Typical of help given to the ground forces was the destruction of a large ammunition dump near this same port. Unfortunately, aircraft were in such short supply that after August 13th Collishaw was forbidden to attack targets on behalf of the ground forces unless an enemy attack was imminent. To pass the time, he devised tactics like flying his one and only Hurricane fighter from airfield to airfield, to mislead the Italians into thinking that there were whole squadrons of these modern aircraft.

The Air Officer Commanding-in-Chief at Cairo, Air Chief Marshal Sir Arthur Longmore, wished that there were. He had just 29 squadrons (some 300 aircraft) in his entire area of responsibility, which included Egypt, the Sudan, Palestine, Transjordan, East Africa, Aden, Somaliland, Iraq, Cyprus, Turkey, the Balkans, the Mediterranean, the Red Sea and Persian Gulf—approximately one aeroplane for each 15,000 square miles.

There were $13\frac{1}{3}$ squadrons in Egypt, plus a few Wellington D.W.I.'s for minesweeping, 1 squadron in Palestine, $3\frac{1}{3}$ in the Sudan, $5\frac{1}{2}$ in Kenya (South African, Rhodesian and local auxiliary units), $3\frac{1}{2}$ in Aden, $1\frac{1}{3}$ in Iraq and 1 in Gibraltar which was transferred to Coastal Command on August 12th. Gladiator biplanes and early Blenheim I's were probably the best of the assortment of combat types, which included Valentia bomber-transport biplanes, based on a 1922 design, Battles, various Hawker biplanes of the Hart family, and Wellesleys, which had proved ideal aircraft for breaking the world distance record but had a maximum bomb-load of only 2,000 lb., carried in underwing containers.

Italy had 282 aircraft in Libya, 150 in East Africa and 47 in the Dodecanese, with little difficulty in sending further squadrons across the Mediterranean as needed. In terms of effectiveness, her two main combat types, the Fiat CR.42 biplane fighter and Savoia-Marchetti SM.79 bomber, were comparable with the Gladiator and Blenheim. Yet the *Regia Aeronautica*, and later the *Luftwaffe*, were destined never to reverse the superiority established by Collishaw's squadrons in the first weeks of the three-year campaign in Africa.

One territorial conquest by the enemy had to be permitted through sheer weight of numbers. Under cover of the R.A.F. and Royal Navy, the 1,500 troops in British Somaliland fought a skilful delaying action before being evacuated from Berbera. As a parting gesture, four Wellesleys of No. 223 Squadron battled through severe icing conditions, over great mountain ranges and past heavy defences to Addis Ababa, to destroy four SM.79's, three hangars and the private aircraft of the Duke of Aosta, Governor-General of Italian East Africa and Viceroy of Ethiopia.

As there were only 19,000 British troops in Somaliland, the Sudan and Kenya at the start of the war with Italy, against 200,000 of the enemy, it was due largely to the air forces that other territorial losses were minute. Ethiopians willing to rebel against their Italian masters were provided with air support and Maria Theresa dollars. Most important of all, the R.A.F. and Royal Navy kept complete control of the Red Sea and its approaches, to such an extent that only one ship was lost from 54 convoys in the second half of 1940.

This was vital. With powerful enemy air and naval forces in the Mediterranean almost all supplies and reinforcements for General Wavell's army in Egypt had to be taken around the Cape. By comparison, it was only a short journey by air or sea from the Italian homeland to Libya. The imbalance was changed a little when Fleet Air Arm Swordfish torpedo-bombers from the carrier *Illustrious* put three of Italy's six battleships out of action in their epic raid on Taranto, on November 11th, 1940; but while Italy remained hostile it was always to be a hazardous and costly business to try to pass Allied convoys through the Mediterranean.

For this reason, Malta assumed from the start a vital importance out of all proportion to its size. Situated a mere 60 miles from enemy air bases in Sicily and utterly dependent on supplies brought from hundreds of miles away, it had seemed so untenable to pre-war defence planners that little attempt had been made to provide the four squadrons of fighters allocated for its defence. Fortunately, the airfields for them and an early-warning radar station had not suffered similar delay.

With passage by sea difficult and air routes over France closed, the only way that aircraft could be flown from the U.K. to the air forces in Egypt was over the Bay of Biscay to Gibraltar and then via Malta. The island was also, clearly, of value as a base for air reconnaissance and as a refuge for naval forces.

The Italians were not unaware of its potential. Within 24 hours of entering the war, they hurled against Malta the full might of more than 200 aircraft based in Sicily. They kept up the attack almost daily for two months. All that Malta could put up initially in the way of airborne defence were four Sea Gladiator biplanes that had been stored in packing cases at Kalafrana as carrier spares. One was knocked out early in the fight. The others, nicknamed Faith, Hope and Charity by the islanders, flew alone against an air force, with such spirit that the Italians estimated that there were 25 of them.

Not until the end of June were four Hurricanes sent to help in the eneven battle. Then, for a month, these seven fighters put up such a defence that the Italians were compelled to make their attacks from a great height in an effort to avoid interception. When this tactic failed, the bombers asked for fighter escort. Finally, they sought the cover of darkness—an admission of defeat in the daylight skies by a defence force now reduced to five aircraft.

Twelve more Hurricanes arrived on August 2nd, flown off the carrier *Argus;* their ground crews and stores arrived by submarine. From that moment the island was secured. It was to suffer grievously from later attacks, particularly by the *Luftwaffe;* but, in turn, it was to strike back harder and harder. Within three days of the arrival at Kalafrana of a pair of Sunderland flying-boats, Flt. Lt. W. W. Campbell of No. 230 Squadron sank two Italian submarines. Marylands of No. 431 Flight and Sunderlands of No. 228 Squadron were responsible for reconnaissance flights that pinpointed the targets for the Fleet Air Arm attack on Taranto; and in December 1940 Malta acquired its first squadron of Wellingtons (No. 148), as the vanguard of a force that was eventually to plague Italian supply lines in North Africa.

Meanwhile, in Africa itself, there had been both triumphs and setbacks for the British forces. An important early development had been the setting up of an air route across Africa by which short-range aircraft could be ferried to reinforce Longmore's units, as only long-range types could follow the Biscay–Gibraltar–Malta route. A base was established at Takoradi in the Gold Coast where aircraft shipped from Britain could be assembled and then flown in easy stages along a 4,000-mile route through Nigeria, French Equatorial Africa and the Sudan to Cairo.

B.O.A.C. navigators were enlisted to guide the early ferry flights and the first formation of six Hurricanes, led by a Blenheim, left Takoradi on September 19th, 1940. It arrived at Abu Sueir, in Egypt, on the 26th, having lost one Hurricane *en route.* By the end of the year, 102 other aircraft had followed them—a trickle that was to grow into a flood numbered first in hundreds and then in thousands.

The reinforcements were sorely needed. At first all had gone well in the desert west of Alexandria. Marshal Rodolfo Graziani, the Italian commander, began the invasion of Egypt on September 10th. On the one and only road, along the coast, a great triumphal arch had been erected, through which Mussolini expected soon to pass on his way to the captured jewel of Cairo, the gateway to all the riches of the east. Instead, it was a disordered mass of Italian soldiery in retreat that went through and around the arch, followed closely by the troops of Major General Richard O'Connor and harassed by aircraft of 202 Group.

Having advanced 60 miles into Egypt in two days, to the village of Sidi Barrani, Graziani had spent six weeks preparing for the next stage. Impatient for a trial of strength, O'Connor attacked on December 9th. Within two months the whole coast of Cyrenaica, as far as El Agheila, was in British hands. Advancing 600 miles, at the cost of under 3,000 casualties, two divisions of troops, supported by 200 aircraft, routed nine Italian divisions and 400 aircraft, took 130,000 prisoners and captured 1,290 guns and 400 tanks. Unfortunately, it was to prove a hollow victory, as the Germans were already coming to the aid of an ally who was proving more of an embarassment than a help.

Malta took the first blows. As 1940 drew to a close, the 75 Italian aircraft remaining operational in Sicily were joined by the 77 long-range bombers, 61 dive-bombers, 22 twin-engined fighters and 12 long-range reconnaissance aircraft of *Luftwaffe Fliegerkorps X*. Against them, the island could muster just one squadron of Hurricanes, two squadrons of bombers and one and a half squadrons of reconnaissance aircraft. There should have been more fighters but, through a tragic miscalculation, eight of the twelve Hurricanes despatched from H.M.S. *Argus* on November 17th ran out of fuel and were lost at sea. Three of those that reached the island had under five gallons of fuel left in their tanks on touch-down.

After a small-scale raid on January 9th, *Fliegerkorps X* showed its real strength next day with a 60-aircraft attack on a British convoy in the narrow seas between Tunisia and Sicily. The main target was the carrier *Illustrious*, which limped badly damaged to Malta. On the 11th, the cruiser *Southampton* was lost in a similar attack, and her sister the *Gloucester* badly damaged. Nobody doubted that the *Luftwaffe* would try to finish off the *Illustrious*. To forestall the onslaught, Wellingtons struck at German airfields; but a concentrated attack on Grand Harbour and the crippled carrier began on the 16th. It was met with fanatical determination by the defences, as were subsequent raids, and on the 23rd the *Illustrious* was able to steam away to safety in Alexandria. The 'Illustrious blitz' was over, with victory to the defenders, but there were plenty more 'blitzes' to come before Malta's ordeal was ended.

Further east, also, the main enemy was changing. In the hope of an early conquest, and to the displeasure of Hitler, Mussolini had invaded Greece from Albania, on October 28th. The Greeks considered themselves perfectly capable of coping with the enemy army, but had only a tiny air force. Much to Longmore's dismay, in view of the expected imminent attack by Graziani, he was ordered to send one squadron of Gladiators (No. 80) and three squadrons of Blenheims (Nos. 30, 84 and 211) to support the Greek army. In addition, No. 112 Squadron, due for re-equipment, handed over its Gladiators to the Greek Air Force, and Wellingtons provided additional support from bases in Malta.

Hampered by having to operate under appalling conditions, from primitive airfields, this small force did its best to aid Britain's new ally. Italian air raids on Athens soon became fewer, and by the end of the year No. 80 Squadron had claimed 42 enemy aircraft destroyed while escorting Blenheims and protecting Greek troops in front-line areas, against six of its own aircraft lost in action.

In January 1941, while the campaign in Cyrenaica was at its height, Longmore was ordered to send No. 11 Squadron (Blenheims), No. 112 Squadron (Gladiators and Hurricanes) and No. 33 Squadron (Hurricanes) to supplement those already in Greece. He complied reluctantly: but there was worse to come.

Hitler could tolerate no longer the thought of Mussolini's 'new Roman legions' being driven back ever deeper into Albania by the forces of a nation as small as Greece. As early as December 13th, 1940, he had issued his first directive for Operation Marita—the occupation of at least the Aegean coast—mainly through fear that R.A.F. bombers might attack the Rumanian oilfields from bases in Salonika. He now began planning a full-scale invasion of Greece and Yugoslavia and by early April had massed 27 German divisions on their borders, supplemented by divisions from Italy, Hungary and Bulgaria, and supported by the 1,200 combat aircraft of *Luftflotte* 4.

The preparations were noted by the British Defence Staff. The advance in Africa was halted and the decision was taken to transfer four army divisions and two more squadrons from North Africa to Greece. No. 113 (Blenheim) Squadron went in March, followed by the Lysanders and Hurricanes of No. 208. This left just one armoured brigade and one semi-trained infantry division in Cyrenaica, supported by four squadrons of aircraft. They comprised Nos. 3 (R.A.A.F.) and 73 with fighters, No. 55 for bomber reconnaissance and No. 6 for tactical reconnaissance.

Little did they realise that their original enemy—very strongly reinforced—was now deploying for a counter-attack side-by-side with the German *Afrika Korps*, including one *panzer* (armoured) regiment, and a full *panzer* division, under the redoubtable Erwin Rommel. In the air, Italian squadrons prepared to strike in company with more than 100 Ju 87 dive-bombers and Bf 110 fighters of the *Luftwaffe*.

The outcome was inevitable. Within nine days of launching their attack, on March 31st, the enemy was again at Bardia, on the border of Egypt. There Rommel stayed, his supply lines stretched to the limit and very conscious of the fact that, to his rear, Tobruk was not only unsubdued but gave every indication of staying that way, with the help of Nos. 6 and 73 Squadrons, which had elected to stay within its perimeter defences.

Heartbreaking though this reversal of fortunes must have been to Wavell, the situation in Greece was even more desperate. While Rommel's tanks were racing across North Africa, on April 6th, a far greater German army swept over the borders of Yugoslavia and Greece. Belgrade quickly suffered the same fate as Warsaw and Rotterdam before it. The numerically-strong Yugoslav army, made up largely of infantry, was devastated and demoralised by the *blitzkreig* tactics of air power and tanks working together with ruthless efficiency.

The R.A.F. squadrons in Greece, under Air Vice-Marshal J. H. D'Albiac, fought gallantly and to good effect. In Eastern Macedonia, 12 Hurricanes providing fighter cover for Greek army units engaged 20 Bf 109's and shot down five without loss. The bombers flew 100 sorties against German communications and columns of troops before the first Blenheim was lost on April 11th. But it was hopeless to expect such successes to continue when, as in Norway, the campaign was already lost on the ground and operations had to be flown from a diminishing number of airfields, all well reconnoitred by the *Luftwaffe*.

When the weather cleared on the 13th, the Blenheims maintained their very effective harassing of German troops, but lost the whole of one formation of six aircraft in the process. On the 15th, near Larissa, all the Blenheims of 113 Squadron were destroyed or damaged on the ground by strafing Bf 109's. Two of a flight of three Hurricanes of 33 Squadron were jumped during take-off and crashed; the third ploughed into the 20 enemy aircraft involved in the attack and shot one down.

Five days later another 12 Blenheims were wiped out at Menidi.

On the 23rd, thirteen Hurricanes were destroyed at Argos. Still the survivors fought on, though it was now only to cover yet another evacuation, to Crete. To the credit of the Royal Navy and the R.A.F., four-fifths of the troops who had been sent to Greece were re-embarked safely and taken to Crete. Blenheims provided air cover for the ships. Sunderlands of Nos. 228 and 230 Squadrons landed in isolated spots on the coast to collect headquarters staff and V.I.P.'s, among them the King of Greece. Little notice was taken of their official capacity of 30 persons, and one Sunderland managed to get airborne with 84, although it took a rather long run before doing so.

The Greek campaign had cost Wavell Cyrenaica, to no avail. It had cost the R.A.F. in Greece 198 aircraft but, against this, some 350 Italian and German aircraft had been destroyed. Unfortunately for the tired soldiers and airmen evacuated to Crete, they had gained but a temporary reprieve. Many had left even their personal weapons on the mainland and the *Luftwaffe* blockaded the island so effectively that they received only 10 per cent of the 27,000 tons of equipment and supplies despatched to them from Egypt in May.

There was little the R.A.F. could do to help. About a dozen battle-weary Hurricanes and Gladiators of Nos. 33, 80 and 112 Squadrons were serviceable on the island, supplemented by a similar number of Fleet Air Arm Fulmar fighters. The Blenheims had gone on to Egypt and Longmore's successor, Air Vice-Marshal A. W. Tedder, felt wisely that there was little point in sending more aircraft to a place that could not possibly withstand an all-out enemy attack when they could be used to far better effect in the forthcoming vital battle for Egypt. The best that could be done was to send over a few Hurricanes now and again to replace losses.

It was soon clear that the end was in sight. Day after day the *Luftwaffe* pounded Suda Bay and anything unfortunate enough to be caught in the approaches to the port. Then it was the turn of the airfields. The Hurricanes and Gladiators fought until further resistance was impossible. How could seven aircraft hold out any longer against *Fliegerkorps VIII*, which was carrying out the softening-up operation, and *Fliegerkorps XI*, which was to be used for the actual invasion? Between them, these German air forces mustered no fewer than 430 bombers, 180 fighters, 700 transports and 80 gliders. The transport aircraft and gliders were to ferry 15,000 airborne troops to Crete, while another 7,000 travelled by sea.

On May 19th the surviving British fighters were withdrawn to Egypt. On the following day the invasion of the island began. The seaborne force was smashed and beaten back by the Royal Navy, after being located by a Blenheim from Egypt. At Heraklion and Retimo, German paratroops were wiped out or driven into retreat by the dogged defenders. Troops who landed by glider at Canea were disposed of quickly. But by sending in paratroops and airborne units at Maleme, under cover of non-stop air attack, the enemy secured the airfield and used it to fly in more than 20,000 troops by the 27th.

Twelve Hurricanes were sent from Egypt to help in the defence of Heraklion. Our own naval gunners shot down two and drove off three more; four of the remainder crashed on landing or were shot up by the enemy before they could play any part in the fighting. Other Hurricanes, based in Egypt, managed to destroy a number of enemy aircraft on the ground and in the air, by using external fuel tanks for the long return flight; but nothing could affect the final outcome of the battle.

By the end of the month it was all over. Nearly 15,000 troops and members of the R.A.F. were snatched to safety by the Royal Navy, under the wings of the *Luftwaffe* and out of effective range of R.A.F. cover. The cost was appalling—three cruisers and six destroyers sunk, 17 other ships damaged, including a battleship and a carrier. Tangible losses to the enemy included 220 aircraft destroyed, more than half of them transports. More significant, perhaps, was that Germany never again mounted a major airborne operation.

The first half of 1941 was not all disaster. The victories seemed small by comparison with the defeats, but were none the less important. In a swift three-months campaign, ending at Addis Ababa on April 6th, the whole of East Africa was regained by armies attacking from the Sudan and Kenya, aided by powerful air support and a seaborne invasion at Berbera. This released six squadrons of the R.A.F. and S.A.A.F. to reinforce those in Egypt. At the same time a squadron of Beaufighters arrived from the U.K.

Meanwhile, on April 3rd, with encouragement and a promise of active help from Germany, a somewhat scurrilous politician named Rashid Ali had seized power in Iraq, with the support of four generals. Fifty miles west of the capital, Baghdad, was the great R.A.F. training station of Habbaniya which, with others at Basra and Shaibah, was operated in accordance with the Anglo-Iraqi Treaty of 1930. When its occupants got up on the morning of April 30th, they discovered that 9,000 of Rashid Ali's troops had installed themselves on a 200-ft. high plateau overlooking the airfield, complete with 28 pieces of artillery.

This was not unexpected.   Air Vice-Marshal H. G. Smart, A.O.C. Iraq, had only three Gladiator fighters at Habbaniya, for advanced training, but the engineering staff had spent 3½ weeks fitting guns and bomb-racks to 70 of the other aircraft of No. 4 Flying Training School.   Each of the Audaxes now had racks for a pair of 250-lb. bombs, representing a vast improvement over the 20-pounders these vintage biplanes had carried in their operational heyday.   The Oxfords were adapted to carry eight 20-lb. bombs. To supplement the flying instructors, the brighter pupils were given immediate promotion to operational status.   Others, together with members of the ground personnel, were accepted as observers and gunners.   The result was christened the Habbaniya Air Striking Force, with a strength of four 'bombing squadrons' and one flight of Gladiators, supplemented by six more flown over from Egypt. Wellingtons of Nos. 70 and 37 Squadrons were detached at the same time from Egypt to Shaibah.

Forestalling any move by Rashid Ali, who could have knocked out the station by shelling the water tower or power station, Smart sent his unique air force into action at 04.45 hours on May 2nd. Preceded by bombs from the Shaibah Wellingtons, the ex-trainers dived on the rebel army from all points of the compass.   It was a lively day, in which Habbaniya's aircraft flew 193 sorties, losing two machines in the air and three on the ground.   They reduced considerably the enthusiasm of the enemy artillery, whose shells had caused more concern than had the attempted intervention by Iraqi combat aircraft.

The battle continued on the 3rd and 4th.   Blenheim fighters of No. 203 Squadron helped to beat off the enemy air force and Iraqi Levies from Habbaniya joined in by creeping up on enemy outposts and artillery-men by night and despatching them by their own specialised and silent techniques.

On the night of the 4/5th, a few of the Audaxes and Oxfords kept up the bombing of the plateau after dark.   It was the last straw for Rashid Ali's troops, who could no longer move up supplies by night. A dawn reconnaissance on the 6th found the plateau deserted.   At once the Habbaniya aircraft took off to harry the retreating enemy. They also caught a column of motorised infantry and artillery moving up as reinforcements and turned it into a solid mass of flame, 250 yards long.

By this time, outbreaks of rebel activity in Southern Iraq had been dealt with by air and land forces, which now linked up with the garrison from Habbaniya for the advance on Falluja and Baghdad. On May 31st it was all over, and not a day too soon for by then He 111 bombers and Bf 110 fighters of the *Luftwaffe* and a squadron of Italian CR.42 fighters had arrived to pose a new threat to British presence in Iraq.

Many units shared in the final victory in Iraq, but the lion's share of glory went to No. 4 Flying Training School. As the R.A.F.'s official historians commented later: 'The rout of an organised army and air force by makeshift crews in training machines, who in less than a month flew some 1,400 sorties against the enemy, was a feat unprecedented in the brief but crowded annals of air warfare.'

There was one more potential trouble-spot in the Middle East that had to receive attention before all efforts could again be concentrated against Rommel's *Afrika Korps*. The German aircraft in Iraq had flown there via Syria, and while this country and Lebanon remained under Vichy French control the enemy clearly had a foothold in an area that could be strategically embarassing, being in the rear of Allied forces in Egypt and close to Britain's sources of oil supply.

On June 8th, 1941, Australian, Free French and Indian troops, supported by the 1st Cavalry Division, 4½ squadrons of R.A.F. fighters and bombers and a tactical reconnaissance flight, began battling their way towards Beirut and Damascus. The Vichy French air and land forces put up a strong fight, and it was not until July 12th that the French asked for a cease-fire. A decisive factor had been the R.A.F. fighter attacks on airfields, which accounted for many of the 55 French aircraft destroyed in the campaign, against the loss of only three British fighters.

Syria, Iraq and East Africa could thus be deleted from the list of immediate worries when the Defence Committee of the War Cabinet met in mid-July. Far greater problems remained on the agenda. In particular, it appeared essential to strike against Rommel's forces in North Africa at the earliest possible moment.

Hitler's obsession with the menace of Communism had culminated in Operation Barbarossa, the German invasion of the Soviet Union on June 22nd. A welcome side-effect of this had been the ending of the 'blitz' against the U.K., as every *Luftwaffe* aircraft that could be spared had been moved to the new eastern front to support the German armies. But, like Hitler, the British War Cabinet did not expect the Russians to hold out for more than a few weeks. Hence the need for haste in Africa, to take advantage of Germany's preoccupation elsewhere.

In Cairo, General Auchinleck had succeeded Wavell. Neither he nor Tedder felt they could guarantee a successful campaign until November, arguing that they expected their strength in tanks and aircraft to double by then. Reluctantly, Churchill agreed to the delay.

In September, the ground forces that were being prepared for the offensive under General Sir Alan Cunningham, were named the Eighth Army. The five squadrons of Wellington bombers in the Canal Zone became No. 205 Group. No. 201, at Alexandria, was redesignated No. 201 (Naval Co-operation) Group. No. 202 Group, with Hurricanes, Wellingtons, Marylands and Bombays, became Air Headquarters Egypt, with responsibility for local air defence. No. 204 Group was officially Air Headquarters Western Desert but was to become immortal as the Desert Air Force. Its purpose was defined as the establishment of air superiority by offensive sweeps, attacks on enemy airfields and use of its own anti-aircraft guns, rather than to provide an umbrella over the army. This represented a tremendous, and vital, advance in the understanding and application of the capabilities of tactical air power.

Less spectacular, but equally important, was the setting up of No. 206 Group by Air Vice-Marshal Graham Dawson of the Ministry of Aircraft Production. Its task was to collect and repair aircraft damaged in action and by the end of 1941 it had 23,000 civilians on its payroll, doing work far beyond the standard that had been considered possible in that part of the world.

Thanks to No. 206 Group and the arrival of new aircraft, Tedder had some 700 aircraft poised for take-off in Egypt and Malta when the count-down for Operation Crusader began on November 18th, 1941. There were nine squadrons in Malta, 11 in the Canal Zone and Delta, and 29 in the Western Desert, under Air Vice-Marshal Arthur Coningham. Facing them were only 283 serviceable German and Italian aircraft; but there were 1,500 more within reach in Tripolitania and on the other side of the Mediterranean.

On the ground, the two sides were fairly evenly matched. Rommel's tanks were far superior to their British counterparts, but a month of non-stop air attacks on his supply lines had left him with only small reserves of everything needed for success in battle. Even worse for him, the R.A.F. had established such air superiority that he was taken by complete surprise when the Eighth Army began its attack, whereas efficient reconnaissance had given Cunningham a very good picture of the disposition of his enemy.

By November 21st, the Tobruk garrison, under siege since Rommel's counter-attack in April, were able to break out and join in the fray. Just as success seemed to be assured, Rommel sent his armoured columns on an undetected race towards the Egyptian border. His bold stroke might have succeeded but for determined opposition by the 4th Indian Division and British mobile columns, and the deadly work of Hurricane fighter-bombers, Blenheims, Marylands and, by night, Fleet Air Arm Albacores, which caught the main enemy column near Sidi Omar.

For three weeks the tide of battle ebbed and flowed like a naval engagement—as well it might, for the desert has much in common with the sea. On December 16th, it seemed that Rommel's forces were finally encircled at Gazala and might be destroyed once and for all. But Coningham could not use his bombers because of the difficulty of identifying friend from foe, and Rommel managed to elude the 7th Armoured Division which had hoped to block his retreat. Harassed day and night by the Desert Air Force, he was back at El Agheila by early January. Once more Cyrenaica was clear of the enemy, with the wrecks of 458 enemy aircraft littering airfields between the Egyptian border and Benghazi, and countless burned out tanks and lorries, to bear witness to the achievements of Coningham's squadrons. But, as in the Spring of 1941, victory was soon to turn sour.

There is no space in a book such as this to trace the whole course of the war in North Africa during the two years that followed. Suffice it to say that by February 14th, Rommel was back at Gazala, almost within sight of Tobruk once again. One reason was that, on December 7th, Japan had attacked Pearl Harbor, bringing the U.S.A. into the war, and was rapidly driving the British forces from Burma and Malaya. With India threatened, there was no alternative to withdrawing men and machines from the Middle East. Another reason was Rommel's masterly tactics in the desert. A third was a reduction in Malta's offensive activities.

Hitler had decided in October 1941 to put a permanent stop to Malta's interference. Between June 1st and October 31st, at least 220,000 tons of enemy ships had gone to the bottom on the supply routes to Africa; of the 115,000 tons sunk by air attack, three-quarters could be credited to R.A.F. and Fleet Air Arm squadrons based in Malta. Nearly half of all the supplies and equipment despatched to Rommel's army in this period was at the bottom of the Mediterranean.

Even operations in Russia had to take second place to Malta for a time, and one of Germany's greatest commanders, General-feldmarschall Kesselring, was transferred from his H.Q. before Moscow to Rome, followed closely by the squadrons of *Fliegerkorps II* which flew to bases in Sicily. A total of 250 German and Italian long-range bombers and reconnaissance aircraft and nearly 200 fighters were now available to smash Malta whose air commander, Air Vice-Marshal H. P. Lloyd, could muster only 60 bombers and 70 fighters.

The storm broke on December 22nd, with the main effort directed against the airfields at Luqa, Hal Far and Takali and the flying-boat base at Kalafrana. Lloyd's Hurricanes fought like tigers, and his Blenheims even hit back against airfields in Sicily; but more than 500 sorties were flown against Malta's air bases in the first few days of January. Simultaneously, heavy rains turned them into quagmires, leaving only Luqa operational. Eventually, the Blenheims had to be withdrawn to Egypt; the Wellingtons and Swordfish that remained took off whenever there was a break in the attack, but sank only one ship in the whole month of February.

As day followed day, the enemy onslaught grew in intensity, but Malta proved as indestructible as London. Its soldiers built pens out of sandbags, petrol cans and rubble to protect the precious fighters. After raids, R.A.F. ground crews toasted their bread over still-burning incendiaries. There were plenty of them, for in February a total of nearly 1,000 tons of bombs fell on the island, and March beat even this record. In the middle of that month, all bombers were withdrawn except for a few Wellingtons; but, on the credit side, Malta had become the first place outside the U.K. to receive Spitfires. There were only 15 at first, to support 30 surviving Hurricanes, but more were to follow.

Up to 218 aircraft now hit Malta each day; the total for March was 2,850 sorties and 2,174 tons of bombs. Sixty of the enemy never returned to Sicily to fight again.

Twice in April, more than 300 aircraft raided Malta in a 24-hour period. Even the island's destroyers and submarines now left to seek safer harbours. But the ordinary people of Malta were still able to cheer the British Commander when he passed, and on the 16th of that month the island was awarded the George Cross—a unique distinction that reflected the bravery of an entire community of civilians and servicemen.

During April, the enemy flew 4,900 sorties against Malta and dropped 6,728 tons of bombs. Of 47 Spitfires flown to the island from the U.S. carrier *Wasp*, on the 20th, only 27 remained intact on the following morning and only 17 by evening—before one of them was ready for action.

Far more serious was that vital supply convoys sent to the island in February and March had been destroyed. It was impracticable even to attempt to reach the island in April and, in Sicily, there were unmistakable signs that the Germans were preparing an airborne invasion of Malta. It never came. In early May, Hitler decided that a high proportion of Kesselring's aircraft would be better employed in the Soviet Union, Cyrenaica and France, and Malta was reprieved.

Under continued but lighter attack, Malta used its time well to prepare for the next round. On May 9th, 62 more Spitfires flew in from the *Wasp*. This time they were not caught with their cowlings open. When enemy aircraft arrived to destroy them, they found the Spitfires waiting in the air and spoiling for battle. A ship-load of ammunition reached the island on the 10th, followed by 17 more Spitfires on the 18th. The staging of aircraft through Malta, *en route* to the Middle East, had never stopped; now her Wellingtons were back to resume their offensive.

They were too late to cut off the supplies for Rommel's next attempt to take Tobruk and the Free French fort at Bir Hakim and to wipe out Cunningham's armour, *en route* to Egypt. But Rommel's thrust failed. Little did Malta realise that success would have signalled the green light for Operation Hercules—invasion of the island.

The time had come to try to break the enemy blockade. On June 13th, a convoy of 11 merchant ships left Alexandria, escorted by cruisers and destroyers and covered by Beaufort, Albacore and Wellington torpedo-bombers from Malta, Beauforts from the Western Desert and Liberator four-engined bombers newly arrived in Egypt—some flown by U.S. Army Air Force crews—with supporting reconnaissance, anti-submarine patrol, light bombing and fighter aircraft.

All this effort was wasted. Non-stop attacks by enemy aircraft, submarines and fast patrol boats quickly sank four of the merchant ships. With a powerful Italian naval force on its way to deal with the rest, the convoy turned back. Sole consolation for Malta was that two of the Italian ships would cause no further trouble, as the cruiser *Trento* was sunk and the battleship *Littorio* badly damaged by Allied air and sea forces.

A second convoy, despatched simultaneously from Britain, received equally rough treatment, but two merchant ships survived to reach Malta on June 16th. The island had been saved, at the cost of a cruiser, five destroyers, two minesweepers, six merchant ships and more than 20 aircraft.

When Kesselring renewed his major offensive in July, Malta was ready. Half of her 200 aircraft were now Spitfires, with a squadron of twin-engined Beaufighters to back them up. After losing 44 aircraft in a fortnight, the German commander again slackened the pressure. He was to make one desperate last fling, in October, when Goering ordered destruction of Malta in eight days, but by then the attackers were frequently fighter-bombers rather than the formidable Ju 88's, and often they were beaten off before even reaching the island. And another supply convoy had got through to the island, at the cost of the carrier *Eagle*, three other ships of the Royal Navy and 18 aircraft. At last, it was clear that Malta was invincible and that the attempt to eliminate her had simply tied up squadrons that might have made all the difference to the crucial battles in North Africa. Yet, the enemy had had little choice in view of Malta's ability to dominate Rommel's supply routes.

For Rommel himself, the day of reckoning was at hand. With another swift master stroke he had eliminated Bir Hakim and Tobruk in June 1942 and swept on into Egypt. But the Eighth Army, while losing 60,000 men, had been allowed to retreat in good order for 400 miles without destruction from enemy ground forces or air attack. True, it had continued to receive powerful air cover; equally clearly, the *Luftwaffe* of 1942 was very different from the highly-professional, confident *Luftwaffe* of 1940. The toll of fighting on too many fronts was beginning to tell.

The place where the Eighth Army reformed, until then too insignificant to appear on many maps, was El Alamein, where the desert narrowed to a gap only 38 miles wide between the coast and the impassable Qattara Depression to the south. An army that con-centrated its forces in such a spot, under capable leadership, might stave off further retreat and have a sound base for attack. The Eighth Army did just this. Having repelled an enemy frontal attack on July 1st (behind which Mussolini waited on a white horse to lead a triumphal procession into Cairo), it found that its own counter-attack led only to excessive loss of its tanks, which were still inferior to those of the enemy; so it settled down to build up its strength until it could overwhelm the enemy by sheer weight of numbers. At the same time, the R.A.F. and Royal Navy redoubled their efforts against the enemy supply lines, with disastrous results for Rommel.

Meanwhile, its high command changed. On August 15th, Auchinleck handed over to General Alexander, while Lt. Gen. B. L. Montgomery took over command of the Eighth Army. Tedder and Coningham remained in control of the air forces, now supplemented by a growing number of Warhawk fighters and Mitchell and Liberator bombers of the U.S.A.A.F., under Major-Gen. L. H. Brereton, as the nucleus of the future American Ninth Air Force.

On October 19th, Montgomery launched his offensive from Alamein under cover of a thousand-gun artillery barrage. He had 165,000 men, 2,275 guns and 600 tanks, against the enemy totals of 93,000, 1,450 and 470 respectively. Tedder had at his disposal 1,500 aircraft, of which 1,200 were based in Egypt and Palestine. They were made up of 60 R.A.F. and F.A.A. squadrons, 13 American, 13 South African, five Australian, one Rhodesian, two Greek, one French and one Yugoslav. Little more than half of Rommel's 689 aircraft were serviceable.

The attack achieved complete surprise. Rommel reacted quickly, but every enemy attempt to reform and counter-attack was broken up by the Allied air forces. Hurricane IID's, each carrying a pair of 40-mm. guns under their wings (as big as Bofors anti-aircraft guns), did particular execution, to such a degree that No. 6, one of the squadrons involved in thus 'opening up' Rommel's tanks, still has a winged can-opener as its unofficial badge to this day. By November 3rd, the enemy were in full retreat and the road west was marked by an ever longer trail of wrecked and burning tanks and vehicles as the Allied air forces encouraged them on their way.

As always, the air forces owed much of their mobility to the skill and devotion of the Royal Engineers, whose task was to keep in pace with the advancing combat forces and ensure that the pilots always had airfields from which to operate. Sometimes entirely new airstrips had to be cleared and levelled; at other times, it was possible to put back into service captured enemy airfields, after dealing with any mines or booby traps left by the late occupants. The newly-formed Royal Air Force Regiment also proved its capabilities as an airfield defence force during this campaign and soon earned a great reputation for courage in ground fighting and skill in anti-aircraft gunnery.

By November 13th Tobruk was in British hands, this time for keeps. On the 19th Benghazi fell. Once again Rommel succeeded in halting the advance at El Agheila—but only long enough to build up sufficient supplies to keep ahead of the Eighth Army in a race across Tripolitania. By January 23rd, 1943, Montgomery's army was in Tripoli and Mussolini's new Roman Empire no longer existed. What is more, the elusive Rommel was now between two fires—the second lit on November 8th by Operation Torch, the landing of an Allied Expeditionary Force, under U.S. General Dwight Eisenhower, in Algeria. The object was to thrust quickly into Tunisia and trap Rommel's retreating armies, with simultaneous landings in Morocco, to eliminate Vichy French footholds in North Africa.

After initial successes, the plan began to go awry. Realising that if the German and Italian forces were driven from the whole of Africa, his 'Fortress Europe' would be wide open to attack through the back door of Italy, Hitler despatched huge volumes of troops, equipment and aircraft into Tunisia across the short air and sea routes from Sicily.

At this stage, all the Allied air forces in the Mediterranean and North Africa were put under the unified control of Tedder, as Air Commander-in-Chief Mediterranean Air Command. They comprised the Royal Air Force Middle East, under Air Chief Marshal Sir Sholto Douglas, Royal Air Force Malta, under Air Vice-Marshal Sir Keith Park, and Northwest African Air Forces, under American General C. Spaatz and including Coningham's units from the Middle East that were harrassing Rommel in the south of Tunisia.

It required four more months of hard fighting to end the war in Africa. At one critical stage, in mid-February, a drive by Rommel on Kassarine went so well that there was a possibility that he might thrust through the mountains of central Tunisia and cut off the whole of the Allied armies in the North. When it failed, Rommel made one last desperate attack on his old enemy, Montgomery, at Medanine. 'Monty's' guns were waiting and the enemy lost 52 tanks. Sick and broken in spirit, Rommel left for Germany. His successors, Von Arnhim in the North and General Messe of Italy in the South, were now faced with an impossible task, but they fought tooth and nail for every inch of ground, particularly at Mareth, which the Eighth Army finally had to outflank by taking to the hills—a hazardous operation made possible only by tremendously heavy and sustained air support.

Still the enemy tried to send in reinforcements. In a single month, 20 German and Italian supply vessels were sunk. Desperately, the *Luftwaffe* tried to fill the gap by the use of Ju 52 transport aircraft and even slow and cumbersome six-engined Me 323 glider-type aircraft. Never had Allied fighter pilots had such sport. Between April 5th and 22nd, a total of 432 enemy transport aircraft were destroyed for the loss of 35 fighters. It was little short of a massacre, especially as the Me 323's were often weighed down with ten tons of petrol which turned them into huge aerial bonfires when lit.

On May 12th Von Arnhim surrendered; what was left of his air force, except for some fighters, had already limped over to Sicily. Next day, Messe followed suit, and Eisenhower's armies began rounding up nearly a quarter of a million prisoners. As Hitler had feared, the back door to Europe was now wide open.

Chapter Five

The Defeat of Germany
September 1941 - May 1945

---

*Not only the British Empire now but the United States are
fighting for life; Russia is fighting for life, and China is fighting
for life. Behind these four great combatant communities are ranged
all the spirit and hopes of all the conquered countries in Europe . . .
Just these gangs and cliques of wicked men and their military or
party organisations have been able to bring these hideous evils upon
mankind. It would indeed bring shame upon our generation if we
did not teach them a lesson which will not be forgotten in the
records of a thousand years.*

Winston Churchill, House of Commons, December 11th, 1941

JAPAN'S ATTACK ON Pearl Harbor, on December 7th, 1941, had
brought the United States finally and openly into the war. As in
the case of Britain's other new ally, Russia, the U.S.A. was to find
itself losing rather than gaining ground initially; but even Hitler
must have shuddered occasionally to think that four-fifths of the
human race were now allied to Britain, however reluctantly. To
add to his worries, as a new year approached, a Soviet counter-
offensive pushed back his troops which had penetrated to Rostov
and the outskirts of Moscow, while the rigours of the Russian Winter
brought to the ill-clad *Wehrmacht* a further reminder of the circum-
stances leading to Napoleon's disastrous retreat from Moscow in
1812.

Churchill, too, had his new worries. Much of the equipment
needed to maintain and increase the effectiveness of Britain's
fighting forces came from across the Atlantic. Initially, it had been
paid for, and the U.S.A.A.F. had good reason to be thankful for the
thriving American aircraft industry that had been built up,
financially and technologically, to meet Britain's needs. Now, the
U.S. Services needed such equipment themselves, in vast quantities,

and as it had been supplied to the U.K. under the Lend-Lease Bill since March 1941, without payment, it might have seemed logical for the U.S.A. to fulfill its own needs first, thereby cutting off the streams of Kittyhawk fighter-bombers, Mustang fighters, Liberator bombers, Catalina amphibians, Boston, Maryland and Baltimore light bombers, and other types that were performing such magnificent service with the R.A.F. in every theatre of war.

In the event, the fear proved groundless. So far as possible deliveries were maintained by a rapid speed-up in production. The target was set at total deliveries of 60,000 aircraft in 1942 and 131,000 in 1943, with delivery to the U.K. in 1943 of 589 heavy bombers, 1,744 medium bombers, 2,745 light bombers, 4,050 fighters, 402 observation aircraft and 852 transports, plus trainers.

The main eventual aim of the Allies in Europe was the invasion and liberation of all the nations occupied by Hitler. Until such time as that became possible, Germany was to be weakened by ceaseless air attack, which seemed also to be the best way of helping the Soviet Union until it was possible to open the 'second front' in France. The plan was for R.A.F. Bomber Command to maintain its night offensive, while U.S.A.A.F. 'heavies', operating in mass-formations, protected by the cross-fire of hundreds of guns, would operate in daylight. It was hoped to base in Britain by April 1943, 17 groups of heavy bombers, 10 groups of medium bombers, 6 of light attack aircraft, 7 of observation and photo-reconnaissance aircraft, 12 of fighters and 8 of transport aircraft.

There was no longer any problem in getting the larger aircraft to the U.K. As far back as November 1940, the R.A.F. had found a way of saving valuable shipping space and eluding the U-boats when a flight of seven Hudsons, needed urgently by Coastal Command, were ferried across the Atlantic by civilian crews led by Captain D. C. T. Bennett of B.O.A.C. From this tiny initial operation had emerged R.A.F. Ferry Command in July 1941. Within 18 months, its pilots were flying 16,000 hours a week. Transatlantic flying had thus become routine and the U.S.A.A.F. now followed the trail blazed by the R.A.F., to build up its 8th Air Force in Britain. Bombers flew direct; fighters via Greenland and Iceland.

While the Americans built up their strength, Bomber Command gradually worked out a formula for increasing its effectiveness. Experience of German night bombing had shown that industrial production was disrupted not so much by the loss of individual factories as by the cutting off of water, gas and electricity supplies, breakdown of communications and absenteeism resulting from destruction of the workers' homes. Weight for weight, it was also clear that incendiary bombs were far more effective than high-explosive types in industrial areas. These lessons gave birth to the policy of area bombing of large industrial centres, in which the greatest possible concentration of bombs was dropped, using a precise aiming point such as a railway station or marshalling yard.

In order to saturate the defences, the attacks were to be concentrated in time as well as area. It remained only to convince the War Cabinet that an offensive on these lines would achieve more than a division and diversion of Bomber Command's effort to the purely defensive war at sea or the support of land forces in secondary theatres.

It was for this purpose that the Command's C.-in-C., Air Marshal A. T. Harris, launched Operation Millennium, the first 1,000-bomber raid, on Cologne, on the night of May 30/31st, 1942.

From 52 airfields, a total of 1,046 aircraft took off and headed for the German city. To make up this number, 367 were contributed by Bomber Operational Training Units and Heavy Conversion Units. The majority of the great stream of bombers consisted still of Wellingtons, Whitleys and Hampdens, but there were 338 Stirlings, Manchesters, Halifaxes and Lancasters.

Since early March, the R.A.F. had been using a new radar navigation aid, known as 'Gee', which gave a position fix within six miles at a range of 400 miles from the transmitters. Unlike the German *Knickebein*, which gave an accurate fix only at the point where its beams crossed, 'Gee' in effect laid an invisible radio grid over the continent, so that a navigator could determine his position at any time. It now brought Harris's great bomber force so close to the target area that the crews had no difficulty in identifying the aiming point in bright moonlight.

Quickly, 898 crews unloaded 1,455 tons of bombs on Cologne, two-thirds of them incendiaries, and the burning city could still be seen when the bombers were 150 miles away, *en route* for home. Only 44 failed to return—representing a loss ratio of 3.6, compared with the usual 4.8 per cent for earlier raids in similar conditions. The defences had been saturated as Harris had predicted. In addition, losses had been reduced by 50 R.A.F. intruder fighters despatched to create diversion and confusion over airfields in Belgium, France, the Netherlands and Germany.

Over 600 acres of the built-up area of Cologne had been destroyed completely. This was nearly as much as the total damage resulting from all previous Bomber Command raids on Germany.   There could have been no greater vindication of Harris's tactics and no more dreadful warning to the German people of what lay ahead for them.   The Prime Minister was greatly impressed, especially when another great raid by 956 aircraft was made on Essen and neighbouring towns in the Ruhr only two nights later.

Such pressure could not be maintained without disrupting training and, in fact, only one more raid by over 1,000 aircraft was made in 1942 (against Bremen on June 25/26th), and no further call was made on Training Units to supplement the main force after September 17th.   It was hardly necessary, for Churchill now allocated to Bomber Command the priorities it needed so desperately. Halifaxes and Lancasters went into service in growing numbers, gradually superseding the earlier 'twins'.   Improved radio and radar navigation aids like 'Oboe' took over when the Germans learned to jam 'Gee' and new weapons of great might were evolved for the 'heavies' to carry.

An ominous new sound was heard over Cologne for the first time on the morning after Operation Millennium, when four Mosquitos undertook the first bombing raid by this type of aircraft.   The idea was to harrass the enemy in his attempts to clean up the city after its ordeal.   Before long, 'Mossies' were specialising in this type of operation, carrying two-ton blockbusters and penetrating as far as Berlin.   Built of wood and powered by two Merlin engines, they were easy to construct, a delight to fly and so fast that they carried no guns, being able to outfly any contemporary enemy fighter.

So great was their effect on Goering and Hitler that, later in the war, introduction into service of the Messerschmitt Me 262 jet-fighter was delayed by a whole year while it was modified into a Mosquito-type fighter-bomber, thereby saving the Allied bomber forces from earlier depredation by an aircraft that might have blunted the daylight offensive and changed the course of the war at a critical period.   Yet, there might never have been a Mosquito but for the persistence of de Havilland and the faith of Sir Wilfred Freeman, Air Council Member for Research, Development and Production, for few people believed in the concept of a 380 m.p.h. unarmed wooden bomber when the idea had first been put forward in October 1938.

Eventually, Mosquitos were to be built in nearly 40 different forms, for a vast range of duties.   Reconnaissance versions had been serving with the P.R.U. since September 1941, bringing back photographs from all over Western Europe, pinpointing enemy warships, airfields, radar stations and other targets, and recording the results of Bomber Command's raids.   German General Baron von Fritsch had said in 1939 that 'The next war will be won by the military organisation with the most efficient photographic reconnaissance.'   The Mosquito, as much as anything, proved him right.

In addition, Mosquitos replaced Beaufighters as the main radar-equipped home-defence night fighters, and then added four 500-lb. bombs to their four cannon and four machine-guns to earn new laurels as fighter-bombers.

Fighter sweeps over France began as early as December 1940. Having little to do after the Battle of Britain had been won, the new C.-in-C. of Fighter Command, Air Chief Marshal Sholto Douglas, sent his squadrons over the Channel to seek out the enemy.   When they went alone in small numbers, the formations were called 'Rhubarbs'; when they operated in great strength, accompanied by bombers, the expeditions were known as 'Circuses'.

In general, the *Luftwaffe* refused to be provoked, and the 104 'Rhubarbs' and 11 'Circuses' flown up to mid-June 1941 cost a total of 33 British pilots, against the claimed destruction of only 26 enemy aircraft.   In the next six weeks, the attacks were stepped up, in an effort to relieve pressure on the Russians following Hitler's invasion of their country.   More than 8,000 offensive sorties were flown by Fighter Command, escorting 374 bombers.   Against a loss of 123 pilots, the R.A.F. claimed the destruction of 322 enemy aircraft.   In fact, there were only some 200 German aircraft in northern France at that time and the real loss to the *Luftwaffe* was 81 fighters.   Nonetheless, the enemy recalled many of his most experienced pilots from Russia to meet this new threat.

Even more helpful to the Russians were the convoys of supplies and equipment despatched to them, at tremendous cost in ships and lives, from August 1941 onward.   The first convoy carried 39 Hurricanes, which were operated for about two months by Nos. 81 and 134 Squadrons, in defence of Murmansk, and then handed over to the Russians.   During this brief spell of collaboration with the Red Air Force, the R.A.F. pilots shot down 16 enemy aircraft for the loss of only one Hurricane in combat.

Coastal Command Catalina flying-boats also operated from Russia at this period of the war, to provide protection for British convoys on the last part of their journey.   Other aircraft covered the ships from Scotland and Iceland, and altogether 111 aircraft from 14 squadrons escorted convoy PQ.18 at various times in September 1941.   Protected also by Fleet Air Arm fighters from

H.M.S. *Avenger*, this convoy claimed three U-boats sunk and 35 enemy aircraft shot down—31 of them torpedo-bombers—but lost 13 of its 40 ships in the process.

Shipping losses were very much in the mind of the British War Cabinet at this time, and during 1942 Bomber Command was compelled to devote nearly 44 per cent of its entire effort (a total of 15,500 sorties) to bombing targets in Germany linked with the war at sea, to minelaying and to attacking ports in occupied countries. But the real burden fell on Coastal Command. In several months, more than half a million tons of Allied ships were sunk by U-boats; but science was now coming to the aid of Coastal as it had to Bomber Command. New and more powerful depth charges were introduced. Then, in July 1942, a Wellington made the first U-boat kill at night by illuminating the surfaced enemy craft with a 24-inch searchlight known as a Leigh Light.

Using A.S.V. radar to track down the enemy, and Leigh Lights to pinpoint them, Coastal Command crews sank so many submarines in the Bay of Biscay that Admiral Dönitz ordered all U-boat commanders to sail through the area submerged both by day and night. This had a serious effect on morale and the *Luftwaffe* tried to help by sending Ju 88 fighters over the Bay to hunt the long-range bombers. This was countered by using two squadrons of Beaufighters to deal with the hunters and by November 1942 the Ju 88's no longer molested the anti-submarine bombers.

In another respect, that month was the worst of the entire war, for 814,700 tons of ships were sunk by enemy U-boats and aircraft. Yet it marked a turning point in the battle. When Air Chief Marshal Sir Philip Joubert, C.-in-C. Coastal Command since June 1941, handed over to Air Marshal Slessor in February 1943, he could look back on the destruction of 27 U-boats in his period of leadership, 19 of them in the last five months. He now had 18 squadrons, some about to be equipped with very long-range Liberators that would be able to close the vital mid-Atlantic gap in which U-boats had been free to operate beyond the reach of land-based aircraft and flying-boats. Even he could not forsee how great a toll of enemy submarines would soon be taken by Coastal Command aircraft using the Leigh Light in conjunction with the latest A.S.V. Mk.III radar.

With a wave-length of only 10 cm., as compared with $1\frac{1}{2}$ metres for the Mk.II, A.S.V. Mk.III ended the ability of U-boats to detect A.S.V. radiation from an approaching Coastal Command aircraft, giving it time to dive. It shared many components with Bomber

Command's new H2S navigation and bombing aid which began to be used operationally in January 1943. Entirely self-contained in the aircraft, it produced a radar map of the terrain beneath the aircraft, showing clearly features such as coastlines, rivers, lakes and towns, even from above heavy cloud.

Almost simultaneously, 'Gee' was superseded by a far more accurate and less easily jammed radar navigation aid known as 'Oboe'. This was still dependent upon ground stations, and had a range of only 350 miles, but it formed an ideal navigation aid for the Mosquitos that were now joining the Pathfinder Force.

Harris had not been in favour of Pathfinders when the idea was first mooted. He objected to having many of the best aircrews taken from operational squadrons and concentrated into an *élite* force that would guide the main force by identifying the target precisely and then illuminating it, so that 'marker' aircraft could drop incendiaries (or sky-marker flares above heavy cloud) as aiming points for the main force. However, led by Group Captain D. C. T. Bennett, late of Ferry Command, the Pathfinders went on to prove their worth, by increasing the accuracy of Bomber Command's attacks. Surprisingly, their losses in doing so were less than 3 per cent in 1942, despite the particular hazards of the work, which sometimes involved spending a very long time in the target area.

It would require a book far larger than this to contain the full story of all that Bomber Command—and Fighter and Coastal Commands—achieved in the final two years of the war against Germany. Some operations are among the familiar epics of military history—like 617 Squadron's brilliant attack on the Möhne, Eder and Sorpe dams on the night of May 16/17th, 1943, at the cost of eight of its 19 crews. Leader of the raid was Wing Commander Guy Gibson, who was awarded the Victoria Cross. Designer of the 'bouncing bomb' which made success possible was Sir Barnes Wallis, whose other wartime products included the 12,000-lb. Tallboy and 22,000-lb. Grand Slam 'earthquake' bombs, largest of the war and carried only by Lancasters.

Less well-known are operations like those mounted by Bomber and Coastal Commands in support of Torch, the invasion of North Africa in the Autumn of 1942. Repeatedly, large formations of bombers attacked Genoa, Milan and Turin, to persuade Mussolini to keep his fighters and anti-aircraft guns at home and to convince the wavering Italian people that the war had gone on long enough. Simultaneously, Coastal Command dealt with the submarines that might have ravaged the invasion fleet, sinking three U-boats, sharing in the destruction of a fourth and damaging 23, for the loss of 17 aircraft—some shot down by trigger-happy British and American gunners.

When Torch had achieved its object, and Africa was secure, Eisenhower prepared for the first stage of the Allied liberation of Europe. Tedder had no fewer than 267 squadrons at his disposal, of which 146 were American and 121 British. Many of the fighter squadrons waited on Malta, whose citizens, having endured much, were now to see the tables turned on their tormentors. There were still about 1,000 serviceable enemy aircraft in Italy, Sicily, Sardinia and southern France, but they were outnumbered and there was no longer much harmony between the men of the *Regia Aeronautica* and their more ruthless do-or-die allies of the *Luftwaffe*.

The Allied assault on Sicily was methodical. First enemy communications were attacked; then, for nine days at the beginning of July 1943, it was the turn of airfields. Next big job was to protect the invasion fleet of 2,000 vessels as it assembled at sea. Finally, on July 10th, as the ships neared the landing beaches, Dakotas of U.S. Troop Carrier Command and 35 Albemarle and Halifax aircraft of Nos. 296 and 297 Squadrons approached the island with 137 Hadrian and Horsa gliders in tow, housing 1,200 men of the 1st Airborne Division. Further west, paratroops of the U.S. 82nd Division prepared to drop near Gela and Licata.

This first Allied airborne operation of its kind was not a conspicuous success. Only 12 gliders, all towed by the R.A.F., touched down in the selected area; 69 of the others ended up in the sea. A follow-up by 107 aircraft, carrying the 1st Parachute Brigade and towing 17 gliders, fared even worse. Arriving in the middle of a duel between the fleet and attacking Ju 88's, 14 of the aircraft were shot down while many others became lost and returned to base.

In other respects, the air side of the operation went smoothly. The opposition was ineffective, and while strategic bombers hammered supply lines in Italy, the tactical air force gave the armies all the close support they could wish for. By the time it was all over, on August 17th, a total of 1,850 enemy aircraft had been destroyed or captured, for the loss of under 400 by Tedder's squadrons.

Italy was next, with the situation somewhat confused following the dismissal of Mussolini and Italy's decision to change sides. It was not to remain confused for long. The Germans showed their feelings for their late allies by sinking the battleship *Roma* with radio-controlled glider-bombs when the Italian fleet sailed way to surrender. Some Italian pilots flew their fighters to Allied airfields and announced their friendly intentions with 'victory rolls'; others elected to fight on with the *Luftwaffe*.

Whichever side they were on, it would make little difference. The *Luftwaffe*, like the *Wehrmacht*, intended to contest every inch of the ground that would bring the Allies nearer their homeland; but Tedder achieved air superiority from the start. He had 3,127 aircraft with which to support the Eighth Army, advancing from the toe of Italy, and the U.S. Fifth Army attempting to gain an advanced foothold by landing at Salerno on September 9th.

The *Luftwaffe* tried its hardest to dislodge the Americans, and achieved notable success against Allied ships of the invasion fleet by attacking them with PC.1400FX and Hs 293 radio-controlled glider-bombs dropped from Do 217's. Allied fighters had to operate at extreme range over Salerno, and for a time the issue hung in the balance; but in the end powerful air support and the imaginative use of airborne troops helped to decide the issue on the ground. On September 16th the British and American armies linked up south of Salerno. Naples was entered on October 1st, by which time U.S. strategic bombers had moved to bases around Foggia, which meant that targets in Germany, Czechoslovakia, Austria, Rumania, Hungary, Poland and France could now be hit from both the U.K. and Italy. From Foggia, too, No. 205 Group of the R.A.F. began mining the Danube, causing heavy losses to enemy shipping.

The *Luftwaffe* could still spring surprises, as it showed on December 2/3rd, when Ju 88's sank 17 merchant ships in a night raid on the port of Bari; but such incidents could no longer affect the outcome of the campaign. Bad weather and the stubborn defensive tactics of Kesselring's troops held up the advance on the ground for several months, during which Eisenhower, Montgomery and Tedder left to start planning another and more important invasion, across the English Channel to France. When the Allied armies entered Rome, on June 4th, they were, therefore, under the supreme command of General Sir H. Maitland Wilson, with General Ira Eaker of the U.S.A.A.F. in command of the air forces.

Just two days later, Operation Overlord was launched against Hitler's Fortress Europe. The preparations for this moment of history had been under way for months, even years. Some of them were all too apparent to the enemy. He could hardly ignore Bomber Command's attacks on his production facilities, communications and morale which, in round-the-clock partnership with the U.S.A.A.F. daylight offensive since 1942, had devastated 26,000 acres in 43 German cities by the Spring of 1944. (Yet German production of weapons, including aircraft, was 2½ times greater than it had been in January 1943.) Nor was it any coincidence that fighter-bomber attacks against rail and other communications targets in France had increased tremendously in the Spring of 1944, or that in two months before June 6th, 21,949 British and U.S. bombers had deluged a total of 66,517 bombs on 80 carefully-selected targets, with the emphasis again on railways.

An invasion was coming, but where? By various subterfuges, Hitler was persuaded to guess wrongly.

There had, in fact, been a great deal of subterfuge, subversion and murky work of various kinds going on for years, veiled in wartime secrecy. Some was straightforward 'cloak-and-dagger' stuff, involving black-painted Lysanders which were operated at night by Nos. 138 and 161 Squadrons, from Tempsford, near Bedford, to drop agents and supplies by parachute to reception committees of the French 'underground'. Occasionally they landed in enemy territory to pick up 'Joes'—a somewhat disrespectful term for prominent people who had good reason to leave or others who had done a spell with the resistance movement and now had important news to pass on or simply needed a rest.

Surreptitious deeds of a different kind were performed by No. 100 Group, under Air Vice-Marshal E. B. Addison, who had led the battle against the *Luftwaffe's* radio beams in 1940. Formed on November 8th, 1943, its task was to 'confound and destroy' and by the middle of 1944 it had 12 very special squadrons.

No. 171 Squadron with Halifaxes, 199 with Stirlings, 214 with Fortresses, and 223 with Liberators operated with radio and radar jamming devices to spread confusion wherever they went. There was a high-power transmitter known as *Jostle* which put out a raucous warbling note, not unlike bagpipes, on the *Luftwaffe's* fighter control frequencies. *Mandrel* and *Piperack* fouled up the enemy's ground and airborne radar sets respectively. Strips of metal foil, code-named *Window*, were dropped in such a way that they produced a host of false blips on enemy radar screens, as decoys to divert enemy interceptors from Bomber Command's raiding forces.

Even more secret were the activities of No. 192 Squadron, which indulged in electronic countermeasures work by despatching Halifaxes, Wellingtons and Mosquitos over Germany to ferret out signals from new enemy radar devices.

Finally, for the 'destroy' part of its job, it had the Mosquitos of Nos. 23, 85, 141, 157, 169, 239 and 515 Squadrons, equipped with *Serrate*, which enabled them to home on emissions from radar sets fitted to *Luftwaffe* night fighters; *Perfectos* which triggered off the identification transmitter fitted to German aircraft, and so betrayed their position; and *Monica* tail-warning radar to give warning of any enemy clever enough to creep up on a 'Mossie' from behind. With such equipment, these aircraft managed to shoot down an average of three enemy aircraft each night, often over the *Luftwaffe's* own bases. This had a grave effect on the morale of enemy night-fighter pilots, whose mission had probably been ruined already by a breakdown in control because of the work of other aircraft of 100 Group.

Luftwaffe fighters tried similar intruder tactics over British airfields, often mixing with a stream of returning bombers and then making their attack as the aircraft began their landing approach. The enemy also never gave up the attempt to renew the air offensive against British targets. In late 1942, the fast and formidable Fw 190 fighter-bomber was used for hit-and-run raids on the British south coast and occasionally penetrated as far as London. The contemporary Spitfires were not fast enough to catch the 190's, but the Hawker Typhoon had just entered service with Fighter Command and, with its maximum speed of 412 m.p.h., soon achieved mastery of the raiders.

About a year later, the *Luftwaffe* launched its 'little blitz' on England, with some 550 aircraft of *Fliegerkorps IX*. Adopting Harris's tactics of using pathfinders and concentrating the attack into a short period, the offensive began on January 21/22nd, 1944, with a raid on London by 95 aircraft. Other attacks followed until April, when they gradually faded out.

Meanwhile, the Typhoon had been evolved into a fighter-bomber, carrying bombs or rockets. With these, it played a major part in the fighter offensive by the Second Tactical Air Force, under Coningham, prior to Operation Overlord; in particular it helped the invasion fleet to achieve tactical surprise by destroying many heavily-defended radar stations along the Channel coast.

Another major contribution to success was Operation Taxable, in which 16 Lancasters of No. 617 Squadron flew a carefully-conceived pattern over the Channel at 3,000 ft., dropping *Window* and circling around 18 small ships towing balloons that produced blips on enemy radar similar to those made by much larger vessels. This operation, over the narrow seas off Dover, and a similar pattern flown by No. 218 Squadron off Boulogne, made the enemy think that the invasion force was approaching the Pas de Calais when, in fact, it was destined for Normandy.

The measure of air superiority that had been achieved by the Allies now became fully apparent. There had been virtually no *Luftwaffe* interference with the assembly of the invasion force, and the selected invasion coastline had been isolated by the destruction of bridges, rail communications and radar; yet in making 200,000 sorties and dropping 200,000 tons of bombs in two months, the losses to the Allied air forces had been no more than one aircraft per thousand sorties.

Lessons of the campaigns in Africa, Sicily and Italy had been well learned. Preceded by paratroops and glider landings, Montgomery's main seaborne invasion force thundered on to the beaches of Normandy, covered by the guns of the fleet and by the air forces which were to fly 14,674 sorties (5,656 British) in the 24 hours of D-Day, for a loss of 113 aircraft. Such was the failure of the *Luftwaffe* at the most decisive moment of the war.

Nearly a year of hard fighting lay ahead and Germany never lost an opportunity to hit back. On June 12th, the first of 7,547 V-1 flying-bombs launched against Britain rasped its way towards London and dived to destruction, taking with it any random target that happened to be below. The first V-2 rocket followed in September—a brilliant achievement but yet another admission of the *Luftwaffe's* impotency which required recourse to unpiloted, inaccurate weapons of attack.

Fighter Command dealt quickly with V-1 over the U.K. The first squadrons of Tempest V fighters achieved particular success, as their cruising speed of 340 m.p.h. was higher than that of other fighters, so that they could accelerate quickly to the flying-bombs' 390 m.p.h. as soon as they spotted one. Altogether, 1,847 of the robot weapons were destroyed by fighters, 1,866 by anti-aircraft guns, 232 by the balloon barrage and 12 by the Navy.

That the attack was not overwhelming, as Hitler had planned, was due to the meticulous work of the reconnaissance squadrons and Central Photographic Interpretation Unit, at Medmenham. Photographs taken over the secret German research station at Peenemunde, on the Baltic, had revealed a tiny aircraft on a ramp, similar to those that were being erected in large numbers on the Channel coast of France. Reports from agents told of experiments with long-range rockets and other reprisal weapons (*Vergeltungswaffe*—hence V-1 and V-2), and plans for a bombardment of London.

Peenemunde was hit by 1,937 tons of bombs from 597 aircraft of Bomber Command on the night of August 17/18th, 1943. From October onward, the launch-sites in France became regular targets for fighter and bomber attack. Because of this the V-1 offensive never developed into more than a nuisance; but, like V-2, it was not finally defeated until the launch-sites were captured by the advancing armies.

The break-out from the beach-head had been delayed initially by Montgomery's caution, in not attacking until he was ready, and by stubborn resistance by the *Wehrmacht*. Main trouble-spot was at Caen. On July 7th, Bomber Command took a hand, laying down a carpet of 2,363 tons of bombs north of the city. Hours afterwards, Allied troops were still rounding up pockets of dazed and helpless enemy troops; but the Germans held on to part of the city. On the 18th, 1,919 British and American bombers unleashed another 7,700 tons of bombs, followed by four more heavy daylight raids in other parts of the beach-head between July 25th and August 15th.

Field Marshal von Kluge, in charge of the enemy armies, wrote in despair to Hitler: 'There is no way by which, in the face of the enemy air forces' complete command of the air, we can discover a form of strategy which will counterbalance its annihilating effect unless we withdraw from the battlefield.' But even withdrawal was not possible, as was soon to be made clear.

On August 7th, von Kluge, working to a plan conceived in great detail by Hitler, sent the remaining 400 tanks of six *Panzer* divisions in a thrust towards the sea that threatened to cut off the tanks of General Patton's U.S. Third Army. They had chosen a sector manned by inexperienced troops and had just broken through the defences when the first rocket-firing Typhoons of the Second T.A.F. appeared on the scene. Against slight resistance, the fighters dived repeatedly on a concentration of 60 tanks and 200 vehicles at Mortain. It was a massacre, and as the enemy fled, he left behind on this part of the front 78 armoured fighting vehicles, 4 self-propelled guns and 50 unarmoured vehicles.

Quick action by the ground forces now trapped the remains of 16 German divisions, nine of them armoured, in a pocket at Falaise. A 'cab rank' system, for ground control of fighter-bombers in front-line areas, had been used successfully in Tunisia. Now the 2nd T.A.F. improved on it, using armoured 'contact cars' to locate enemy targets and call in by radio the streams of Typhoons, Spitfires and Mustangs.

In an action typical of many, the Typhoons trapped one long enemy column by first knocking out the armoured vehicles at the front and rear, in a narrow lane, and then methodically destroying with rockets and cannon-fire every vehicle and everything that moved. The scene of destruction there, and throughout the whole Falaise area, was complete and terrible. The Battle of Normandy was over; Montgomery's patience had been justified and Patton's tanks were already rumbling off towards the Rhine.

In the north, Montgomery had a more difficult task. In an effort to end the war before Christmas, he by-passed some strongly-held enemy 'fortresses', such as Le Havre, Boulogne, and Calais, leaving them to Bomber Command and other Allied bomber forces. Despite Hitler's orders to fight to the bitter end, each surrendered after a few days.

In an effort to outflank the enemy's heavily-fortified Siegfried Line, Montgomery took the bold step of dropping paratroops and putting down glider-borne troops at Grave, Nijmegen and Arnhem in Holland, on September 17th, to capture the vital bridges over the Maas, Waal and Neder Rijn. No fewer than 3,887 aircraft and 500 gliders made up the armada, but 1,240 of them were supporting fighters and 1,113 bombers. There were too few transport aircraft to carry in one lift all the troops needed for success, and by the time the second lift reached Arnhem it was too late.

The men on the ground fought like tigers. The crews of R.A.F. Transport Command—formed by amalgamation of six transport groups at home and overseas on March 25th, 1944—earned the new Command its first great and glorious battle honour. Some crews were still throwing out supplies to the doomed airborne forces on the ground when their blazing Dakotas hit the ground after tracing a long fiery trail over the battle-zone.

Failure at Arnhem condemned the Allies to fight on into the new year. Meanwhile, Alexander had lost eight of his divisions from Italy to take part in Operation Dragon, the invasion of Southern France on August 1st. It was worthwhile, for the Allied armies, with strong air support, advanced so quickly that contact was made with Patton's Third Army, at Avallon, on September 12th. Inevitably, the weakened armies in Italy took time to break through the Gothic Line, north of Florence, but they still succeeded in over-running the north Italian plain, to Turin, Milan and Venice, before the war ended.

Also on the southern front, the Balkan Air Force, formed in June 1944 with eight squadrons, one flight and men from five nations, flew 11,600 sorties into Yugoslavia, enabling a quarter of a million guerrillas to tie up 20 German and Bulgarian divisions that would have been an embarrassment elsewhere.

Simultaneously, two South African Liberator squadrons, No. 148 (Special Duties) Squadron and No. 1586 (Polish) Special Duty Flight operated on 22 nights in August and September 1944, carrying arms and ammunition to General Bor's gallant little Polish Home Army which had risen in an attempt to expel the enemy from Warsaw when the Soviet armies were within sight of the city. Not until it was too late would the Russians collaborate by letting U.S.A.A.F. aircraft from the U.K. land at airfields that had been available all the time; Bor's uprising was smashed and the Mediterranean Allied Air Forces had sacrificed for nothing 31 of the 181 aircraft that had tried to help. It was a grim warning that Allies in war might not be Allies after victory—and Churchill for one did not overlook it.

On the main Allied front, Field Marshal von Rundstedt had one final fling on December 16th, 1944. Smashing a path through the American lines in the Ardennes, he tried to repeat the tactics he had used against the French in his breakthrough in 1940. A rapid defensive swing by Montgomery and Allied air superiority ended such hopes within nine days. The *Luftwaffe*, too, made a final appearance *en masse* on new year's day, when between 790 and 870 aircraft, led by experienced navigators in Ju 88's, made a spectacular low-level—and therefore undetected—sweep over 2nd T.A.F. bases, destroying 144 British aircraft alone.

At a cost of well over 200 of their remaining aircraft, the enemy had taught the too-complacent Allies a lesson, for fighter-bombers had been parked wingtip-to-wingtip on some 2nd T.A.F. airfields. The operation achieved no more, at a time when factories in the U.S.A. and U.K. were turning out some 10,000 aircraft every month.

Of technical, rather than operational, importance is that both the R.A.F. and the *Luftwaffe* had been using jet fighters since the summer of 1944. First to go into action, in squadron service, on July 27th had been the Gloster Meteors of No. 616 Squadron. Employed initially against V-1 flying-bombs, with considerable success, they were transferred eventually to France, but never met in action their German counterparts, the Me 262's.

The latter, armed with 30-mm. cannon and air-to-air rockets, achieved a few notable successes against Allied bomber formations, but were too late to turn the tide of the air offensive. By October 1944, opposition had become so insignificant that Bomber Command was able to make daylight attacks on Germany in strength, using Halifaxes, Lancasters and Mosquitos. Oil was now the primary objective and in November 14,312 of the immense total of 52,845 tons of bombs dropped from 15,008 aircraft of Bomber Command hit oil targets.

Germany slowly ground to a halt, short of fuel and short of oil. This the bombers had achieved. Also, at a critical period of the Battle of the Atlantic, they had kept the battle cruisers *Scharnhorst* and *Gneisenau* bottled up in Brest for many months; later, No. 617 Squadron had sunk with 12,000 lb. bombs the mighty battleship *Tirpitz* which had defied the efforts of every other kind of attack.

Bomber Command had demonstrated the terrible power of conventional (as opposed to nuclear) warfare at Hamburg, between July 24th and August 3rd, 1943, when 8,621 tons of bombs, dropped from 3,095 aircraft, created such a conflagration that the city was swept by a fire-storm that burned 6,000 acres and killed 41,800 people. With the U.S.A.A.F., it had compelled Germany's aircraft industry to concentrate more and more on defence, until by 1944 fighters accounted for 78 per cent of all production, bombers only 11 per cent. The bomber offensive also tied up some two million men and women, including 900,000 anti-aircraft gunners, who might otherwise have performed more aggressive duties. Yet, there are still those who suggest that the bombers had little influence on the course of the war. In doing so, they decry the achievements of a Command that lost 47,293 men in the longest continuous battle of World War II.

Figures of men killed, bombs dropped, aircraft built and shipping sunk in the war are so astronomical as to be almost meaningless. The British Commonwealth (originally Empire) Air Training Scheme produced 137,739 pilots and other aircrew in Canada, 88,022 in the U.K., 27,387 in Australia, 24,814 in South Africa, 10,033 in Rhodesia and 5,609 in New Zealand.

Coastal Command had also achieved much, sinking 188 U-boats and 343 ships, totalling 513,804 tons, and protecting countless thousands of Allied ships, so that Britain would never be starved of food or the weapons with which to win the war that had once seemed lost. Transport Command, though new, had played a major part in the last twelve months of the war, not least during the highly successful airborne assault over the Rhine on March 24th, which had signalled the beginning of the end of the war in Europe.

Now, on May 8th, 1945, Field Marshal Montgomery was accepting the unconditional surrender of Germany. Only Japan remained to be beaten, and the Pacific seemed remote to the crowds that gathered to celebrate VE-Day in London.

Chapter Six

The War Against Japan December 1941 - August 1945

No American will think it wrong of me if I proclaim that to have the United States at our side was to me the greatest joy. I could not foretell the course of events. I do not pretend to have measured accurately the martial might of Japan, but now at this very moment I knew the United States was in the war, up to the neck and in at the death. So we had won after all.

Winston Churchill, *The Second World War, Vol. Three*

BACK IN 1920, the Japanese had asked the British government to provide an Air Mission, composed of experienced R.A.F. personnel, to train the Imperial Japanese Naval Air Service up to the standards appropriate to a major air power. Headed by Captain The Master of Sempill, the Mission went to Japan in 1921 and did its work well—too well!

Most members of the British party were ex-R.N.A.S. and, therefore, highly enthusiastic about the potential of torpedo-bombing. They took with them a variety of contemporary British training and combat aircraft, including six Sopwith Cuckoo torpedo-bombers, and soon found their IJNAS pupils to be of 'distinctly high average ability as pilots'.

After the return of the Mission, nobody outside Japan thought much about that nation's military aviation. Reports of the war in China implied that the Japanese had some quite effective fighters and bombers, but it was assumed that most of them were inferior copies of British or American designs. Stories by U.S. newspapermen of the high quality of the 'Navy Zero' fighter used against the Chinese in 1940 were regarded as exaggerated. When more reliable details reached the Air Ministry from other sources in Chungking, the information was transmitted to Air Headquarters in Singapore, but never arrived. A second report was received there, translated from Chinese and, presumably, put in a file for study on some future occasion which never came.

How tiny are the incidents that can change the course of history . . .

Nobody in 1941 doubted the strategic importance of Singapore as a naval base, or that it would be a primary target of the Japanese if the war spread to the Pacific. The Chiefs of Staff in London went so far as to lay down that by the end of that year the strength of the R.A.F. in the Far East should consist of 336 modern combat aircraft, with adequate reserves, ready to operate anywhere from Hong Kong to Calcutta and Ceylon. The authorities in Singapore thought that 566 was a more realistic figure than 336. The old proverb about the road to hell being paved with good intentions was never more apt.

On December 7th, 1941, the Japanese Navy devastated the U.S. Pacific Fleet at Pearl Harbor, using torpedo-bombing and dive-bombing tactics that had been learned first in 1921, coupled with the element of surprise. In Malaya on that fateful day, the C.-in-C., Air Chief Marshal Sir Robert Brooke-Popham, had just 362 aircraft, of which 233 were serviceable.

He, too, was due for a surprise when he tried to match his four squadrons (No. 243 R.A.F., No. 488 R.N.Z.A.F., and Nos. 21 and 453 R.A.A.F.) of American-built Brewster Buffalo fighters against the Japanese Zero. At 10,000 ft. his aircraft had a maximum speed of 270 m.p.h., compared with the Zero's 315 m.p.h., and even this performance had been made possible only by replacing the original armament of two 0.5-in. machine-guns by two of 0.303-in. calibre. The Buffalo was heavy, underpowered, had a slow rate of climb and lacked the agility of its enemy counterpart.

The great danger to Singapore was believed to be from a seaborne invasion; so its big guns all pointed seaward and its offensive air power included two squadrons (Nos. 36 and 100) of antique Vildebeeste biplane torpedo-bombers and three Catalina flying-boats of No. 205 Squadron. There had been another flying-boat squadron, but it was transferred to the Middle East in 1940. The Chiefs of Staff explained to Brooke-Popham that they had intended to replace the Vildebeeste with Australian-built Beauforts, but that production was behind schedule and, anyway, the air forces in the Middle East, and the Russians, had to be given priority in military supplies.

In the event, when the attack came, it was overland from the north, not from the sea. So the big guns were more useless than the Vildebeeste.

Most valuable of all Brooke-Popham's aircraft were the Blenheims of Nos. 27, 34, 60 and 62 Squadrons, R.A.F., and the Hudsons of Nos. 1 and 8 Squadrons, R.A.A.F. The Dutch Air Force could add to the overall total nine Buffalos and 22 Martin B-10 bombers. Japan had 300 modern land-based aircraft in Indo-China, plus her large carrier-borne air forces.

When a Hudson of No. 1 Squadron spotted two huge Japanese convoys of merchant ships and warships sailing west, something over 300 miles from Malaya, on December 6th, there was no longer much doubt that war was near. It came two days later, when Kota Bharu in the north, on the Thailand border, was shelled from the sea and Singapore received its first bombing attack.

It appeared at first that an intended Japanese invasion had been thwarted at Kota Bharu, as Hudsons of No. 1 Squadron sank one of the eight transports that had arrived off the coast, severely damaged two others and killed some 3,000 enemy troops caught in landing barges. In fact, the enemy was soon to be back in greater strength, after landing his main force in Thailand, whose government immediately surrendered.

At this stage, the British bombers should have been directed against enemy aircraft massing at Singora and Patani in Thailand. Instead they were used against the new landing force at Kota Bharu. One Blenheim pilot, his aircraft on fire, dived it into a packed landing barge. The ground forces fought with equal courage; but it was all in vain. Furthermore, the enemy aircraft from Thailand now struck first, against the R.A.F. airfields at Sungei Patani, Penang, Butterworth and Alor Star. Up to 60 fighters and bombers attacked each base, using fragmentation bombs that destroyed machines and men but left the airfields relatively unscathed, for immediate use after the British had been driven out. Such was the degree of enemy confidence and planning.

By evening, only 50 of the original 110 British aircraft in northern Malaya remained airworthy. At last, permission was received to strike back at the enemy in Thailand and on the 9th, a successful raid on the packed airfield at Singora was made by the surviving Blenheims of Nos. 34 and 62 Squadrons, reinforced by another Blenheim squadron. As the same aircraft took off from Butterworth for a follow-up attack, they were bombed and machine-gunned by Japanese aircraft. Only one staggered into the air. Badly wounded, and under continuous attack, its pilot, Flt. Lt. A. S. K. Scarf, did his best to reach the target alone; but he was able to get only as far as the Malay border before landing and dying a few hours later. He was awarded the first Victoria Cross gained in Malaya.

Courage alone cannot win wars. When Singapore had been bombed, its fighter pilots were ordered to stay on the ground, leaving defence to the guns. It probably made no difference. The Buffalos at Alor Star were unable to operate against their attackers as their guns would not work.

The situation deteriorated rapidly. On December 10th, the two most powerful units of the Far Eastern Fleet, H.M.S. *Prince of Wales* and H.M.S. *Repulse*, venturing to sea without air cover, were sunk by Japanese torpedo-bombers whose pilots pressed home their attacks through intense anti-aircraft fire. On the same day, it was decided to evacuate the northern airfields. Only two Blenheims and six Buffalos were still capable of flying from Butterworth.

Pilots of the Buffalo squadrons did their best to provide some sort of air cover for retreating troops, but it was hopeless. Five Japanese aircraft were shot down near Ipoh, but losses were soon so high that the fighter squadrons were ordered to restrict their activity to reconnaissance.

Meanwhile, over the sea, Borneo was captured on December 26th; Hong Kong had surrendered on Christmas Day. Neither had any aircraft to defend them. Singapore now had 75 bomber and reconnaissance aircraft and 28 fighters, following the arrival of six Hudsons and seven Blenheims. Fifty-one crated Hurricanes were said to be on the way. They arrived on January 13th and went into action on the 20th, destroying eight of a formation of 27 Japanese bombers which ventured over Singapore unescorted. Next day, Japanese bombers appeared with an escort of Zeros which promptly shot down five Hurricanes. They might not have done so had not the British fighters, diverted from Egypt, been fitted with sand filters which reduced their speed by 30 m.p.h.

Day after day, the bombing continued and all the time the enemy advanced nearer the island. Even the Vildebeeste pilots braved the Zeros in trying to sink landing craft off the coast; but it was a lost cause and on January 15th the Air Force was ordered to withdraw to Sumatra, except for eight Hurricanes and the six remaining Buffalos which were to cover the evacuation. They did so with great courage, but many ships were lost and the transfer to Sumatra offered only a temporary reprieve for those who got there.

Singapore surrendered on February 15th. Meanwhile, Blenheims and Hudsons evacuated to Sumatra, and reformed as No. 225

(Bomber) Group, were busy escorting convoys and attacking airfields in Malaya from which they had operated themselves a few weeks earlier. Their insecurity was demonstrated when the Japanese bombed Palembang on January 23rd and then dropped paratroops on Sumatra's main airfield, known as P.I, on February 14th. After that, the bombers could operate only from P.II, a secret airfield, when they detected and attacked the Japanese fleet of 25–30 transports, escorted by naval vessels and aircraft, that had been despatched to occupy Sumatra.

In their first attack on the convoy, the bombers sank or badly damaged six of the transports, for the loss of seven of their number. On the 15th, accompanied by Hurricanes, they not only defeated entirely the enemy attempt to land, but killed thousands of Japanese troops and destroyed a number of Zeros on the ground on Banka Island. It was too good to last. The enemy sent more paratroops and the air force had to move on once more, to Java. Soon, three Japanese convoys were heading for this final stronghold of the Dutch East Indies. The bombers fought them to the end, one of their greatest actions being an attack on the convoy that had sunk the entire fleet of the gallant Dutch Admiral Karil Doorman on the 27th. In company with American B-17's, they sent 15 enemy vessels to the bottom; many more were sunk on March 1st. Even after the enemy were ashore, the Hurricanes of 232 and 605 Squadrons continued trying to defend Batavia and attacking Japanese ground forces, wingtip-to-wingtip with Dutch Kittyhawks and Buffalos. The surviving Vildebeeste joined in raids on a captured airfield, until none were left. On March 8th, the uneven struggle ended when the Dutch army commander surrendered.

There remained Burma which, had a defence plan materialised, would have been defended by 280 aircraft. In fact No. 221 Group, with H.Q. at Rangoon, deployed just 16 Buffalos of No. 67 Squadron and 21 P-40's of the American Volunteer Group—the legendary 'Flying Tigers'. Under their commander, General Claire Chennault, the Tigers were normally based at Kunming, to defend the Burma Road, but had been allowed by Generalissimo Chiang Kai-Shek to go in search of some action over Rangoon. They did not have to wait long. Some 400 Japanese aircraft were waiting to spearhead the drive into Burma, and Rangoon suffered its first attack on Christmas Eve. By Boxing Day 221 Group had claimed 36 of the raiders. Soon afterwards, it received the best possible Christmas present of about 30 Hurricanes and a squadron of Blenheims.

The newcomers quickly made their presence felt, by dropping 11,000 lb. of bombs on Bangkok airfield; 58 enemy combat aircraft were destroyed, and dozens more were shot down during the first two months of 1942, when the Japanese raided Rangoon 31 times by day and night and, at the same time, made a bold bid for air superiority. They never succeeded in this, and the Allied air forces only retreated northward because the armies they were protecting had to fall back under overwhelming enemy attacks. Their final success came on March 21st, when ten Hurricanes and nine Blenheims from the civil airport at Magwe caught 50 enemy aircraft on the ground at Mingaladon, destroying 16 on the airfield and 11 of those that took off to fight.

This was too much for the Japanese, who sent no fewer than 230 aircraft to eliminate Magwe. A few British aircraft escaped to Akyab, only to be subjected to a non-stop bombardment for three days. This brought to an end the air battle in Burma.

At this stage, the unarmed Dakotas of No. 31 (Transport) Squadron and the U.S.A.A.F. 2nd Troop Carrier Squadron entered the picture, flying many thousands of civilians to safety and dropping vital supplies to the retreating armies and countless refugees streaming north towards the Imphal Plain and Naga Hills.

With the coming of the monsoon, the enemy halted at the frontier of India. Almost his only failure in five months of incredible conquest had occurred further south, where an attempt to emulate the success of Pearl Harbor at the naval base of Trincomalee had been beaten off. Nonetheless, as Admiral Nagumo withdrew eastward in mid-April, he could look back with satisfaction on the fact that his carrier-borne aircraft and surface vessels had sunk 23 merchant ships north of Ceylon, as well as the carrier *Hermes*, cruisers *Dorsetshire* and *Cornwall* and destroyer *Vampire*.

What he did not know was that, paradoxically, his successes helped to ensure Japan's ultimate defeat. He had lost so many aircraft to Ceylon's Hurricanes and Naval Fulmars that three of his carriers had to return to Japan to refit and so were unable to participate in the Battle of the Coral Sea, the first ever fought entirely by carrier-based aircraft operating against opposing ships. Furthermore, the loss of many of his most experienced pilots may have affected the outcome of the subsequent Battle of Midway, on June 4th, when the Japanese Navy lost four of its finest carriers, restoring the balance of naval power in the Pacific and marking the turning point of the war.

In India, the Supreme Commander Far East Forces, General Sir Archibald Wavell, fresh from his successful campaign in North Africa, spent the second half of 1942 building up his forces for the return to Burma. By the end of the year, his Air Commander, Air Chief Marshal Sir Richard Peirse, had a total of 1,443 aircraft. They were divided among 221 Group, which was responsible for bomber and reconnaissance operations on the Burmese front and over the Bay of Bengal; 222 Group at Colombo, with responsibility for the Indian Ocean and its islands; and 224 Group, controlling the fighters in Bengal and Assam.

Blenheim IV's and American-built Vengeance bombers had re-equipped the three light bomber squadrons evacuated from Burma; other types in service included Hurricanes, some Wellington night bombers, Beaufort torpedo-bombers, Hudsons and Catalinas. To them, in mid-January 1943, were added a flight of radar-equipped Beaufighters which shot down five enemy bombers in two nights and ended Japanese enthusiasm for bombing Calcutta.

Wavell's first small offensive, aimed at the reoccupation of Akyab, did not succeed, but in February 1943 Brigadier Orde Wingate led the first expedition by his Chindits, or Long Range Penetration Group, deep into central Burma, behind the enemy lines. In four months, during which his force was supplied entirely by air, Wingate destroyed four bridges and cut railway tracks in more than 70 places. Equally important, he dented the confidence of the enemy troops, who had considered that only they had mastered the jungle well enough to get away with such activities.

Once more the monsoon season was used to build up strength, and by the end of 1943 there were 49 squadrons with modern equipment that now included three squadrons of Spitfire VC's, five new squadrons of Hurricane fighter-bombers for ground attack, and Liberators for long-range bombing and reconnaissance. No less important had been enlargement of the transport force, which was now in a position to carry whole divisions into battle and keep them supplied solely by air in combat areas.

By the beginning of 1944, all Allied forces in this area had been grouped as South East Asia Command, under Admiral Lord Louis Mountbatten, with Peirse as Air Commander. Against his 64 R.A.F. and 28 U.S.A.A.F. squadrons, the enemy could deploy some 750 aircraft, about half of which were in Burma. With two squadrons already flying 419 m.p.h. Spitfire VIII's, Peirse felt confident of retaining air superiority, and so it was to prove.

First, however, the Japanese made one last, skillful and powerful attempt to overrun the Imphal Plain and break through to India. From February 4th until April, three Japanese divisions kept up the pressure, but the Allied armies stood firm, supplied by air, while reinforcements were flown in to Imphal and to relieve Kohima. They received close support from Peirse's fighters—and, indirectly, from the long-range Lightning and Mustang fighters of the U.S. squadrons which made heavy attacks on Japanese advanced airfields in March and April.

Between the two phases of the Japanese offensive, Wingate had led another army of Chindits into the jungle in the enemy's rear. This time his initial force of 9,052 men, 175 ponies, 1,183 mules and 227 tons of stores was carried 150 miles behind the lines on board Dakotas and gliders, which landed on strips hacked out of the jungle under the noses of the enemy by U.S. engineers and British troops. The construction party had even used bulldozers, landed by glider, without their presence ever being suspected by the Japanese.

Each Chindit column included an R.A.F. officer, who directed fighter-bombers by radio on to targets that the Chindits wanted removed and selected landing sites for the little L-1 and L-5 ambulance aircraft in which Colonel Philip Cochran's Air Commandos evacuated casualties.

A second Chindit brigade followed the first on March 23rd. Next day, the U.S. transport aircraft in which Wingate was travelling crashed in a storm and he was killed. But his work went on, and more than 5,000 enemy troops had died by the time the Chindits withdrew in August 1944.

Between March and June, the Japanese had lost 30,000 men and nearly 100 guns in northern Burma, in trying to hold on to their gains at Kohima and Imphal. Now, despite the onset of the monsoon, Mountbatten decided to give them no rest as they retreated. To reduce sickness in the Allied forces as they advanced through 'malaria country', the Hurricanes divided their time between bombing the enemy and spraying D.D.T. along the roads.

By early November, the Allied armies were over the Chindwin river, and three separate thrusts now developed. From Myitkyina, Stilwell's American–Chinese Northern Combat Area Command headed south through the North Shan States. In the centre, the 14th Army commanded by General Sir William Slim set out for Mandalay and Rangoon. In the south-west XV Corps advanced in Arakan towards Akyab. By establishing complete air supremacy from the start, the Allied air forces made it possible for the 300,000 men of these armies to be supplied with all the food and ammunition they needed by the 17 squadrons of the Combat Cargo Task Force and six squadrons of the Air Cargo H.Q. of the U.S. Tenth Air Force.

Akyab was occupied without opposition on January 2nd, 1945, and the prescribed task of XV Corps was accomplished. Under heavy air cover, it next made an amphibious assault on the mainland at Myebon, followed by a second at Ramree Island, both against intense opposition. It now became a race to capture Rangoon before the monsoon arrived. Mandalay fell on March 20th and on May 3rd the 26th Indian Division, part of XV Corps, landed from the sea and entered Rangoon without a fight. A few hours later the monsoon broke.

The war in Burma was not quite over, as large numbers of enemy troops had been by-passed near the Sittang Bend and planned to break out and find safety in Thailand in early July. Their fate was sealed by Burmese guerrillas and Thunderbolt fighter-bombers, adding more than 10,000 to the tally of 100,000 Japanese killed in Burma.

Nor should the contribution to victory made by the Liberator long-range bomber squadrons be overlooked. The Japanese relied on some 5,000 miles of railways to bring up their supplies, the most famous stretch being the 244-mile line from Bangkok to Moulmein, built at a cost of the lives of 24,000 Allied prisoners-of-war. During the critical first four months of 1945, four squadrons of Liberators were making round trips of up to 2,800 miles to deprive the Japanese of the use of these railways. Using Azon radio-controlled bombs, they became particularly adept at destroying bridges. The enemy, never lacking ingenuity, devised light locomotives that could run both on track and overland, and sometimes built up to three reserve bridges over ravines in vital sectors. Despite such efforts, the tonnage carried by rail from Bangkok dropped from 750 to 150 tons a day.

Britain intended to send troops and aircraft to invade the Japanese homeland, but still had to liberate Malaya, Singapore and other territories beyond. The best Churchill could offer the Americans was three divisions for the main assault and 400 heavy bombers. They were never needed, for the atomic bombs dropped on Hiroshima and Nagasaki in August brought World War II to an end, through the unconditional surrender of Japan. Instead, there was the job of transporting home the survivors of the men who had fallen into the hands of the Japanese as prisoners-of-war.

In 5½ years, the Royal Air Force had grown into one of the mightiest Services in history, with 9,200 aircraft and 1,079,835 R.A.F., Dominion and Allied officers and airmen, of whom 193,313 were aircrew. At its peak, the Women's Auxiliary Air Force was made up of 181,909 women in R.A.F. blue, plying more than 80 trades. For those who lived through it all, *Per Ardua ad Astra*, their motto, had a special meaning when the bells pealed out their message of final victory on August 15th, 1945.

Ready and waiting. Hurricane Is of No. 17 Squadron dispersed along the perimeter of Croydon Airport, on September 3, 1939.

EUROPE
eptember 1939
to 1941

First R.A.F. aircraft to cross the German frontier in World War II was a Blenheim IV of No. 139 Squadron on a photographic reconnaissance sortie from Wyton (Hunts.). This machine had been standing by at Wyton since September 1, 1939, its function being to reconnoitre and photograph the German fleet in its North Sea bases. Picture shows the relevant entry in the unit's Operations Record Book. [*I.W.M.*

(*Page.—220.) W3. 20,310—1577. 14,000. 12/38. T.S. **447**

Appendix Appendix H   R.A.F. FORM

OPERATIONS RECORD BOOK.

DETAIL OF WORK CARRIED OUT.

From hrs 3 / 9 / 39 to 2359 hrs. 3 / 9 / 39   By 139 Sqdn.   No. of pages used for day 1 .

Aircraft Type and No.	Crew.	Duty.	Time Up.	Time Down.	Remarks.	References
Blenheim Mk. IV 6215	F/O McPherson. Cdr. Thompson. c/2 Arrowsmith	Photo. Reco.	1200.	1650.	Duty successful. 75 photos taken of GERMAN fleet. The first Royal Air Force aircraft to cross the GERMAN frontier.	

Left: During the early months of the war the Blenheims, Wellingtons and Hampdens of Bomber Command were employed on daylight armed reconnaissance over the North Sea and along the north-west German coast, whereas the night-flying Whitleys—much to the disgust of their crews—were given the task of dropping propaganda leaflets over Germany. Here a crew-member of a Whitley V of No. 102 Squadron demonstrates how the bundles of leaflets, or 'Nickels' as they were code-named, were dropped down the flare chute.

[*I.W.M.*

Left: Tail gunner of a Whitley V. The power-operated Nash and Thompson tail turret, first installed in the Mark IV and mounting four O.303-in Brownings, provided the Merlin-engined Whitleys with the most vicious tail sting of any bomber in service in 1939—and for a long time afterwards. However, the worst enemy of the Whitley crews on their long and lonely flights during that first winter of the war was not enemy fighters (they rarely materialised), or flak (which was not yet a real threat) but the weather—a hazard trebly formidable in the absence of reliable cockpit heating, electrically-heated clothing, and oxygen apparatus usable in all positions.

Right: An R.A.F. corporal points out bullet holes in the tail of the Heinkel He 111K which was shot down by Spitfires of Nos. 602 and 603 Squadrons on October 28, 1939, during the *Luftwaffe* raid on the Firth of Forth. It crash-landed close to the village of Humbie, on the Lammermuir Hills near Dalkeith, and was the first German aircraft to be brought down on British soil in World War II.

Above left: *Luftwaffe* air base at Langen-haagen, ten miles north of Hanover, photo-graphed by an R.A.F. reconnaissance aircraft in 1939. A, quarters; B, railway line; C, station and platform; D, hangars; E, motor transport; F, oil patches; G, servicing tarmac; H, runway; I, aircraft moving off. Most of the aircraft are Heinkel bombers; two are Ju 52/3M bomber-transports.

[*I.W.M.*

Below left: Avro Anson of No. 502 Squadron, Coastal Command, circles a convoy in the North Atlantic, making sure that all is well. The Anson, or 'Faithful Annie' as the type was affectionately known, equipped eleven squadrons of Coastal Command at the outbreak of war. On September 5, 1939, an Anson of No. 500 Squadron from Detling (Kent) made the first R.A.F. attack of the war on a U-boat. The Anson—which was the first R.A.F. aircraft to have a retractable undercarriage—was eventually supplanted in Coastal Command by the Lockheed Hudson.

Above: Side gunners of a Sunderland flying-boat on coastal patrol off the west coast of England. The Sunderland had also power-operated nose and tail turrets—it was the first British flying-boat so equipped — and some models had mid-upper turrets and/or additional guns mounted in the bows. Because of its strong defensive armament it became known to the Germans as the 'Flying Porcupine'.

[*I.W.M.*

Maintenance of flying-boats like the Sunderland (No. 210 Squadron aircraft illustrated) often meant working in windswept lochs, clinging to a rocking surface poised thirty feet or so above icy, choppy water.   [*I.W.M.*

Wedding ring Wimpey.   When the Germans introduced the magnetic mine at the end of October 1940, British scientists discovered that this type of mine, which blew up when it came into contact with the magnetic field of a passing ship, could be exploded from the air by an aircraft capable of setting up a similar field.   The Wellington seemed to be the most suitable aircraft for the job and some were fitted with a 40-foot diameter duralumin hoop-shaped casing all round them and secured to their nose, wings and tail. Inside the casing was a magnetic coil, and current to it was supplied by an auxiliary engine, of the ordinary Ford V.8 type, carried in the Wimpey.   In January 1940 several Wellingtons of Coastal Command were minesweeping around our shores and this hazardous and unpleasant work continued for about four months, after which it was no longer necessary, ships having been fitted with degaussing gear which rendered the mines ineffective.

A Lysander reconnaissance aircraft taxies in for servicing at an Air Component airfield in France during the bitterly cold winter of 1939-40. In November 1939 a 'Lizzie' shot down the first Heinkel bomber to fall in B.E.F. territory, while in June 1940 Lizzies of No. 4 Squadron gained the distinction of being the last Air Component aircraft to remain in action before leaving for England—their role being to shoot up German positions. [I.W.M.

Airmen of a Battle day-bomber unit warm themselves by a fire in a truly arctic setting at an A.A.S.F. airfield in France during the first winter of the war. [I.W.M.

Working in such conditions was no joke. This picture of airmen of No. 226 Squadron pushing a Battle into its hangar was taken at night when the temperature registered $42\frac{1}{2}$ degrees of frost. It was the coldest spell ever known in France and the men were given rations of rum to enable them to carry on with their work.   [*I.W.M.*

Game of draughts in progress at an R.A.F. billet in France.   [*I.W.M.*

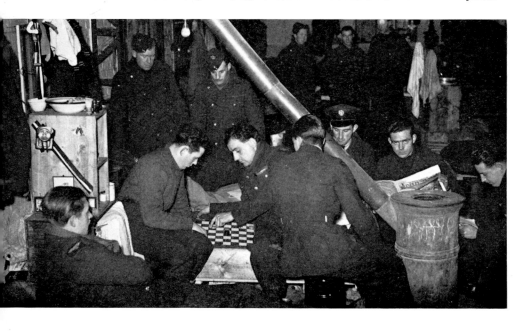

Blenheim IVs of No. 139 Squadron, A.A.S.F., on their way to reconnoitre the Maginot Line during the 'phoney' war. In the opening stages of the Battle of France, 139 Squadron was decimated but after the French collapse it re-formed in Britain in time to operate its 'new' Blenheims against Hitler's invasion barges during the Battle of Britain. [*I.W.M.*

Gloster Gladiators and crews of No. 615 Squadron in France during the 'phoney' war. This unit, and No. 605 (Gladiator) Squadron, served with the Northern Air Component of the B.E.F. and saw action during the Battle of France in May and June 1940. R.A.F. Gladiators also served in Norway and the Middle East, and during the Battle of Britain they equipped No. 247 Squadron at Roborough, charged with defending the Royal Naval dockyards at Plymouth. [*I.W.M.*

Above: Gladiators of No. 263 Squadron on Lesjaskog frozen lake, in central Norway, April 1940. On learning that British fighters were operating in Norway, the Germans made repeated attacks on the lake on April 25 and ten Gladiators were destroyed. Next day the four machines that remained airworthy were flown north to Aandalsnes where, without adequate fuel to continue operations, they were destroyed. *[photo courtesy Air Cdre. Whitney Straight*

Left: Bomber Command was not allowed to drop bombs on German soil during the early months of the war, as the British Government was concerned about the risk of reprisals if casualties were caused among the civil populace. On March 16, 1940, however, a British civilian was killed on the island of Hoy, in the Orkneys, during a German bombing attack on the Fleet anchorage at Scapa Flow; so three nights later Bomber Command Whitleys and Hampdens retaliated by bombing a German land target for the first time—the minelaying seaplane base at Hörnum on the Island of Sylt. Photo shows the crew of a Hampden being greeted on their return from Sylt.

Below: Whitley Vs of No. 77 Squadron at Driffield, Yorkshire, in April 1940. Whitleys of this unit, sometimes operating from an advanced base in France, and frequently doing so in sub-zero weather conditions, penetrated as far as Vienna, Prague and Warsaw on leaflet raids during the 'phoney' war. They subsequently took part in such notable 'firsts' as the first attack on an enemy land target (Hörnum, March 19/20, 1940), the first big attack on the German mainland (the exits of München-Gladbach, May 11/12, 1940) and the first attack on Italy (Fiat works at Turin, June 11/12, 1940).

Low-level attack by Battles on an enemy column of horse-drawn vehicles during the German invasion of France in May, 1940. German troops run for cover across the fields to the right. [*I.W.M*

Lockheed Hudson of Coastal Command approaches Dunkirk on reconnaissance patrol, June 1940, during the evacuation of our forces. The smoke from burning oil tanks forms a suitably dramatic background to the picture. [*I.W.M.*

Barrage balloons over London.
[*I.W.M.*

Hurricanes of No. 85 Squadron on patrol above the clouds during the Battle of Britain. By September 15, 1940 there were 32 Hurricane squadrons in the U.K. and by the end of that month three more had joined the ranks of the defences. During the Battle the Hurricane was employed principally against the German bombers, which seldom operated above about 17,000ft—its own rated altitude being just over 15,000ft— while the faster climbing Spitfire tackled the escorting Messerschmitts which approached at a higher altitude.
[*I.W.M.*

Above: Spitfire I of No. 1 Squadron being re-armed in September 1940 at Duxford Cambs.   [*I.W.M.*

Left: Boulton Paul Defiant two-seat fighters of No. 264 Squadron flying in formation. After some early successes in 1940, the Defiant proved no match for enemy single-seat fighters and from August 1940 it was employed as a night fighter. In this role, equipped with Air Interception radar, it did remarkably well during the winter of 1940-41 but by the spring of 1942 it was being relegated to target-towing.   [*I.W.M.*

Above right: Pilots' summer. Vapour trails left in the sky during a dog-fight over Kent between R.A.F. fighters and enemy aircraft trying to get through to London in September 1940.   [*I.W.M.*

Right: Operations room at H.Q. Fighter Command, Bentley Priory, in 1940. The officers on the dais look down on the W.A.A.F. plotters with their croupier-like sticks at the map table.   [*I.W.M.*

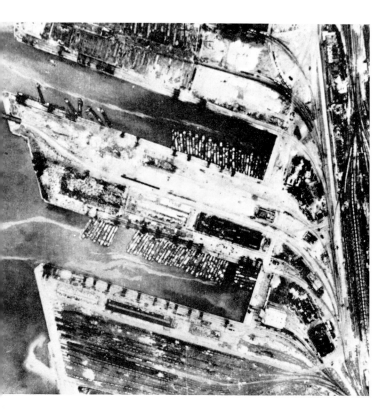

German invasion barges at Dunkirk in the summer of 1940. Dock buildings, unloading cranes, warehouses, wharves, roads, and rail sidings are destroyed or damaged.   [*I.W.M.*

Dornier Do 177s over the Beckton gasworks during a daylight raid on London on September 7, 1940. White stripe on upper starboard wing-tips indicates that they belonged to *1 Gruppe*.
[*I.W.M.*

Secret of success. The control and reporting system in which the Royal Observer Corps played key role, made possible success in the Battle of Britain. Shown is a CH (Chain Home) station of the early RDF (Radio Direction Finding) system first revealed as radiolocation in June 1941. Its official description as a Radio Detection and Ranging system led to the abbreviation—radar.

[*I.W.M.*

Two members of the Royal Observer Corps scan the skies for enemy aircraft from their lookout post. Men and women from all walks of life volunteered for duty with the R.O.C. during the war. All over Britain Observer posts were manned in a continuous day and night service, watching for the approach of enemy aircraft and plotting their course as they flew overhead. R.O.C. members identified every aircraft, Allied or enemy, estimated their speed and height and worked in close liaison with the R.A.F. in transmitting air raid warnings.

[*I.W.M.*

Above: Sqn. Ldr. (now Grp. Capt.) Douglas Bader, the legless R.A.F. fighter ace, photographed in September 1940 when commanding No. 242 Hurricane Squadron at Duxford. [*I.W.M.*

Below: When this Messerschmitt 110 crashed on the South East coast in August 1940, another *Luftwaffe* aircraft tried to bomb it to prevent it from falling into British hands. But the bombs fell wide, the nearest about 20 yards from the target. Here a soldier and a policeman examine the damage. In the background can be seen wooden posts set up to stop landings by enemy gliders. [*Fox Photos*

Left: Cockpit of a Spitfire I.

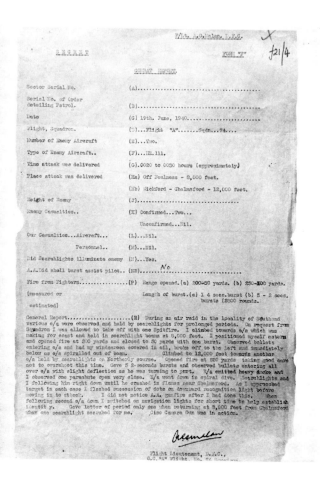

A combat report of Flt. Lt. (later Grp. Capt.) A. G. 'Sailor' Malan, the South African ace, dated June 19, 1940, when he was flying with No. 74 (Spitfire) Squadron. [*I.W.M.*

Hurricane Is of No. 312 (Czech) Squadron. The R.A.F. in the war years was composed of many nationalities. Personnel from the Dominions and Colonies served side-by-side with those from the German-occupied countries. Apart from general service in purely R.A.F. units, R.C.A.F., R.A.A.F. and R.N.Z.A.F. squadrons served under overall R.A.F. command and special Belgian, Czech, Dutch, Greek, Norwegian, Polish and Yugoslav squadrons were formed within the R.A.F. In fact, squadron numbers 300-399 and 400-499 are reserved to this day, as several of our wartime allies and Commonwealth countries respectively still perpetuate their original R.A.F. squadron numbers in their present Services.

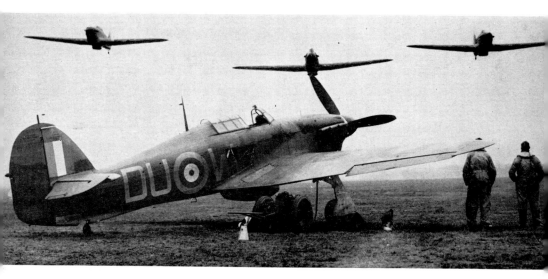

King George VI and Queen Elizabeth, escorted by Air Chief Marshal Sir Hugh Dowding, A.O.C.-in-C. Fighter Command, during an informal tour of the Command's Headquarters at Bentley Priory in 1940. 'Stuffy' Dowding, as he is affectionately known in R.A.F. circles, gained ever-lasting fame as leader of 'The Few' in the Battle of Britain.

[*I.W.M.*

Below:

Got yer! Men of the Home Guard practice how to deal with low-flying aircraft at a training camp in the north of England in September, 1940. No prizes for identifying their target!

Above: Beaufighter IF of No. 604 Squadron equipped with Air Interception radar, in 1941. The 'Beau' was the first really effective night fighter of World War II, supplanting the original AI-equipped Blenheim IF, which lacked the necessary speed and fire-power. Another major role in which the Beaufighter made a great name for itself was that of strike fighter.

Right: From defence to offence. in late 1940 'rhubarb' sorties by day fighters and 'intruder' sorties by night fighters were begun, followed in January 1941 by the first of many joint bomber/fighter 'circus' operations. Pictured here is a Westland Whirlwind of No. 263 Squadron, a type which was eminently suited to 'rhubarb' operations, because of its concentrated cannon fire-power.
[*I.W.M.*

Above: Black-painted Hurricane IIC night fighter/intruders of No. 87 Squadron, led by Sqn. Ldr. D. C. Smallwood in BE500 *Cawnpore I,* photographed during the winter of 1941-42.

[*Charles E. Brown*

Right: Navigator/bomb aimer at his prone position in the nose of a Douglas Havoc night-intruder of No. 23 Squadron at Ford, Sussex, in the winter of 1940/41. No. 23 Squadron specialised in night intrusion over France, and its special three-seat fighter-bomber Havocs were known initially as 'Moonfighters'.

Above: Spitfire VBs of No. 92 Squadron, early in 1941.
[*Charles E. Brown*

Left: Spitfire pilots of No. 43 S q u a d r o n — the famous 'Fighting Cocks'—wearing their 'Mae Wests', wait for an emergency call in their hut at Drem airfield, Scotland. [*I.W.M.*

Blenheim IV of No. 101 Squadron—code letters deleted by wartime censor—watches
the end of an enemy tanker as, ablaze from bows to stern, she sinks in the Channel off
the French coast.   [*I.W.M.*

Above: First official take-off of the Gloster Whittle E.28/39, Britain's first jet aircraft, powered by the famous W-1 gas-turbine engine invented by Air Commodore Sir Frank Whittle. The place and date: Cranwell, May 15, 1941. At the controls was the late Gerry Sayer, Gloster's chief test pilot.

Right: Several types of aircraft served as aerial ambulances during the war. One of these was the Airspeed Oxford ('Oxbox'); others included the Bristol Bombay, the de Havilland Rapide and the Lockheed Hudson. Two Oxford air ambulances were presented to the R.A.F. by the Girl Guides of the Empire and our picture shows some of the donors cheering one of these machines as it flies overhead.

Below: Ground crew load a 'tin-fish' into the racks of a Bristol Beaufort at a station of R.A.F. Coastal Command in July 1941. The Beaufort saw action over the North Sea, the English Channel, the Atlantic and the Mediterranean. F/O Kenneth Campbell of No. 22 Squadron was posthumously awarded the Victoria Cross for his gallantry in a torpedo attack in a Beaufort against the battleship *Gneisenau* in Brest Harbour on April 6, 1941; the attack nearly sank her and kept her out of commission until the end of the year.

Below: Many of the American-built aircraft supplied to the R.A.F. in World War II were flown across the Atlantic by R.A.F. Ferry Command, which was inaugurated in November 1940, and quickly became the largest air transport organisation in the world. R.A.F. personnel and civilians— Americans, Britons and Canadians were included among many nationalities—worked side by side. Our photo shows Lockheed Hudsons being serviced for the transatlantic hop at Gander, the vast terminal in Newfoundland. The U.K. terminal was Prestwick.

W.A.A.Fs at work. A
the outbreak of war th
Women's Auxiliary A
Force was 1,734 stron
and had only five trad
groups. In 1943, whe
the force was at its pea
strength, 181,909 wome
wore the blue uniform c
the R.A.F. and by VE
Day they plied more tha
80 trades, including thos
of flight mechanic, fitte
electrician, radar mechani
and wireless mechanic
Here a W.A.A.F. corpora
gets out target maps fc
the Briefing Room at
bomber station. [*I.W.M.*

On long, highly-polishec
tables at an R.A.F. bombe
station, W.A.A.F. safet
equipment workers pacl
parachutes. For this job
a constant warm, dr
temperature must be
maintained, to keep the
silk in perfect conditior
and to ensure that the
'chutes will open easil
when required. [*I.W.M.*

fty perch. W.A.A.F.
ght mechanics at work
one of the engines of
Sunderland flying-boat.
[*I.W.M.*

rsnip answering E for
ward . . .' W.A.A.F.
eless telephonists in
Watch Office at an
.F. station give return-
bombers permission
land. [*I.W.M.*

Interior of the Operations Room at Bomber Command H.Q., with Air Marshal Sir Richard Peirse (A.O.C.-in-C. from 1940 to 1942) and his staff planning the night's operations. Deep underground, at Naphill, High Wycombe, Bucks, the room—which is still in use today—is lofty, quiet and suffused by a soft light shining from half-concealed reflectors. Its walls are lined with huge maps, charts and blackboards.   [I.W.M.

Ops. Room at a bomber station in England. Here the operations ordered by Bomber Command H.Q. were worked out in detail. 'What is the best route to the target?' 'How can it be identified?' 'What of the weather?' [I.W.M.

'And your vegetables will be planted here'. Bomber Command Stirling crews being briefed for a minelaying or 'gardening' mission. Bomber and Coastal Commands laid mines up and down the shores of Europe to an extent which, by 1945, virtually immobilised coastal shipping. As a result of mines laid by the R.A.F., 759 German-controlled vessels of all types (excluding U-boats) with a total tonnage of 721,977 tons were sunk in North-West European waters during the war. [I.W.M.

Wellington ICs of No. 149 Squadron, *circa* June 1940. The Wimpey, together with two other 'twins', the Hampden and Whitley, bore the brunt of Bomber Command's night offensive during the early years of the war. [Charles E. Brown

Hampdens of No. 16 O.T.U. From the O.T.U.s Bomber Command crews destined for four-engined bombers were posted to the Heavy Conversion Units, where they trained on aircraft of the same type that they would fly subsequently in the squadrons. Sometimes aircraft and crews from the O.T.Us. and H.C.Us. were detailed for operations with the main force.

[*Charles E. Brown*

Fine study of a Halifax I of No. 76 Squadron. The Halifax was the second of the four-engined 'heavies' to enter Bomber Command service in World War II—the first being the Stirling. Although much improved in its later, radial-engined, versions it was never as effective, from any point of view, as the Lancaster. Nevertheless it did much valuable work and became standard equipment of Nos. 4 and 6 Groups, although most of the latter's squadrons eventually re-equipped with Lancasters. The machine illustrated was flown by Plt. Off. Christopher Cheshire, younger brother of the famous Leonard Cheshire, V.C., and was eventually lost in a sortie against Berlin on August 12-13, 1941.

[*I.W.M.*

'One of our aircraft is missing'. Wreckage of a Wellington of Bomber Command shot down by the Germans while bombing targets in North Germany *circa* April 1941. Note the inflated dinghy. During the war a total of 8,655 aircraft of Bomber Command were reported missing on operations and another 2,054 were destroyed or damaged—1,604 of them due to enemy action. (These figures do not include casualties suffered by aircraft on loan to Coastal Command).

As the R.A.F. expanded in World War II, not only did great tracts of countryside give way to vast new airfields, but many stately homesteads were compulsorily requisitioned and transformed into headquarters, billets and the like. One of the many impressive country seats that echoed to the footsteps of R.A.F. personnel was Heslington Hall, York, home of the late Lord Deramore; this late Victorian redbrick and stone neo-Tudor building became the headquarters of No. 4 Bomber Group and today forms part of York University—minus the lovely statue of Ceres which was destroyed in a students' prank.

Cat on the prowl. A Consolidated Catalina of No. 210 Squadron. The Catalina entered R.A.F. squadron service early in 1941 and two V.Cs were won by Cat pilots—one of them by F/O J. A. Cruikshank of 210 Squadron. On May 7, 1945, a Catalina of 210 Squadron was responsible for destroying the 196th and last U-boat sunk by Coastal Command—120 miles North-East of Sullom Voe.

[*Aeroplane*

Breakfast time for men who have been resting 'off duty' during a Coastal Command Catalina's long hours of patrol.

[*I.W.M.*

In August 1941 a British fighter Wing—No. 151 Wing, comprising Nos. 81 and 134 (Hurricane) Squadrons—was sent to Vaenga in North Russia to demonstrate the Hurricane to Russian pilots and ground staff, and to help the Russian Air Force resist the German drive against Murmansk through Norway and Finland. Before returning to Britain at the end of 1941 the Wing handed over its aircraft and equipment to the Russians. Photo shows a Russian soldier guarding a Hurricane at Vaenga.
[*I.W.M.*

Scene at an Elementary Flying Training School in Britain in the winter of 1940/41. While instructors and pupils await their turn to fly, an Anson comes in to land and a Tiger Moth takes off. [*Aeroplane*

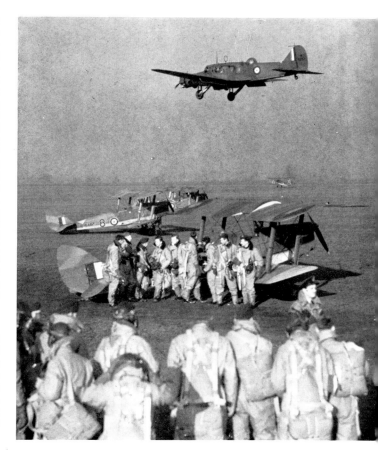

W.A.A.Fs at a Scottish station of Flying Training Command
prepare a Miles Master for a night sortie.   [*I.W.M.*

Flying classroom.   An instructor trains wireless operator
trainees inside a Dominie, the specially-equipped service
version of the Rapide, over the English countryside.

A vast contribution to the growth of the R.A.F. in World War II was made by the Empire Air Training Scheme, later called the British Commonwealth Air Training Plan. It was in operation from May 1940 to March 1945, during which period it established in Canada alone no fewer than 360 schools and kindred units. (Above) an R.C.A.F. Anson I of No. 1 Air Observers' School over the snow-covered Canadian landscape in March 1941. (Below) three Harvards on a formation practice flight from the Advanced Training School at Cranbourne, Rhodesia, *circa* September 1941. [*lower photo I.W.M.*

Above: Airmen install a camera in a Lysander of Army Co-operation Command before a reconnaissance sortie. Army Co-operation Command was formed in December 1940 from No. 22
Army Co-operation Group, and its function was to organise, experiment and train in all forms
of co-operation between the R.A.F. and the Army. Squadrons of this Command came under
the operational control of the Army and, including those attached to armoured divisions, had a
mobile organisation housed in vans which could be moved at short notice. Following the
experiences of tactical air forces in the Western Desert and North Africa, Army Co-operation
Command was merged into the 2nd Tactical Air Force, within the organisation of Fighter Command,
in June 1943.

Right: Paratroops and a supplies container leave a Whitley of No. 1 Paratroop training school,
Ringway, Manchester. The Whitley played a major role in the training of Britain's 'Red Beret'
army from scratch, although it was far from ideal as a dropping vehicle. In February 1941 Whitleys
carried the paratroops who destroyed the *Acquedetto Pugliese* at Tragino in southern Italy
(Operation *Colossus*) and in January 1942 they carried those who stole the *Wurzburg* radar
apparatus from the German radar station at Bruneval on the French coast.   [*I.W.M.*

Below: R.A.F. pilot pupils study aircraft recognition at an Elementary Flying Training School.
[*I.W.M.*

Wellesley, probably from No. 47 Squadron, above the strange landscape of Eritrea, on its way to attack Keren. On June 11, 1940, the first day of the East African campaign, Wellesleys of No. 14 Squadron operating from Port Sudan destroyed 350,000 gallons of petrol on the Eritrean airfield of Massawa. Wellesleys were withdrawn from day-bombing operations in late 1941, but were used subsequently for shipping reconnaissances, under No. 201 Group, until February 1943.   [*I.W.M.*

MIDDLE EAST

Blenheim I roars over the heads of British troops on patrol in the Western Desert.   [*I.W.M.*

Paratroops of the Special Air Service of the British Army enter a Bristol Bombay bomber-transport for a practice jump in the desert. The Bombay served with three squadrons in the Middle East in mid-1940. Some of No. 216 Squadron's machines were hurriedly fitted with bomb racks and used on night-bombing raids against the Italian forces from Sidi Barrani to Benghazi. Later, Bombays evacuated troops from Greece and, in November 1941, undertook the first airborne operation in the Middle East when 54 paratroops were dropped at Tmimi in Libya. [I.W.M.

Night attack on Benghazi seen from a British bomber. The zig-zag patterns are caused by anti-aircraft fire, while the white blobs are bomb explosions. [I.W.M.

A Martin Maryland reconnaissance bomber returns to its desert landing ground after a lone flight over enemy territory, while ground crew service one of its sister ships. The Maryland was the first American bomber to be used by the R.A.F. in North Africa and its most famous operation was, perhaps, the reconnaissance of the Italian Fleet at Taranto before the Fleet Air Arm attack of November 11, 1940. It was used also by the South African Air Force.

[I.W.M.

Italian cruiser *San Giorgio* on fire after a bombing raid by the R.A.F. on Tobruk harbour on the night of June 12/13, 1940. Burned out and beached, the vessel remained in use as a flak-ship in spite of much subsequent attention from Allied aircraft.

[I.W.M.

To speed up vital supplies of fighter aircraft to the Middle East air forces, a scheme was inaugurated in the latter part of 1940 whereby the machines were disembarked at Takoradi on the Gold Coast, in West Africa, after a sea journey from England, and then uncrated, assembled and flown in stages to Egypt. The air journey of 4,000 miles was one of variety and hazard, but after an inauspicious start the Takoradi route became firmly established. By May 1943 over 5,300 British and American aircraft, including not only fighters but also light bombers, transports and other types, had been flown from Takoradi to the Middle East Command. Picture shows a Hurricane being removed from its crate for assembly at Takoradi. [*I.W.M.*

Blenheim I of No. 211 Squadron returns to its base in Greece after a raid against Italian positions in Albania late in 1940. [*I.W.M.*

Arab Legion guards watch the unloading of a Vickers Valentia of No. 216 Squadron at an Iraqi airfield during the rebellion in May 1941. At that time five Valentias and five Bombays of 216 Squadron were engaged in transporting troops and ammunition into Iraq.   [*I.W.M.*

R.A.F. personnel being rowed out to one of the Sunderland flying-boats which did such a magnificent job during the withdrawal from Greece in May 1941.   [*I.W.M.*

German Ju 52/3M paratroop transport plunges to its doom during the invasion of Crete in May 1940

[*I.W.M.*

Low-flying Hurricane IIC escorts lorries of a New Zealand unit on the move in Egypt early in 1942.

Above: Tank-buster. Hurricane IID of No. 6 Squadron in the Western Desert. The twin 40-mm guns of the IID were capable of automatic or single-shot fire and wrought havoc on Rommel's tanks, armoured fighting vehicles and transport in the Western Desert and North Africa.   [*I.W.M.*

Above right: Some of the troops who worked on Malta's airfields, making pens for aircraft, altering and maintaining landing grounds and refuelling, leave a dispersal point for their mid-day meal.
[*I.W.M.*

Below right: Army Bren gun carrier brings trolley loads of bombs to a Wellington II at Luqa, Malta, *circa* December 1942.   [*I.W.M.*

Below: Curtiss Kittyhawk IA of No. 112 'Shark' Squadron, having landed during a sandstorm at Sidi Haneish airstrip, Egypt, is guided to its dispersal by a mechanic sitting on the wing. [*I.W.M.*

Left: Spoils of war. An R.A.F. pilot with some war trophies, including an Italian officer's hat, in the Western Desert.   [*I.W.M.*

Below: This wilderness of wrecked aircraft was left behind by the retreating enemy at Castel Benito air-field, 14 miles from Tripoli.   [*I.W.M.*

Among the large number of enemy aircraft which fell into Allied hands during the Eighth Army's advance in the Western Desert were many which, although damaged, were made serviceable and test flown for technical intelligence purposes. A captured Ju 87D Stuka undergoes repair. [*I.W.M.*

Combined R.A.F. and Army wireless observation unit in Libya. Known to the men as 'Wous', these units did a fine job during the desert campaign. [*I.W.M.*

Troops board a Hudson of the Western Desert Air Transport Service in the spring of 1943. The Air Transport Service facilitated every stage of the Army's advance, bringing up a constant stream of troops and vital supplies. Several types of aircraft were used, from medium transports such as the Hudson to the large Bombays and DC-3s. Aircraft which flew fresh troops forward often returned with the wounded, some of the machines being specially adapted to take stretcher cases.

[*I.W.M.*

Hurricane tank-buster attacks enemy armour with machine-guns and cannon during the closing stages of the Tunisian campaign.

[*I.W.M.*

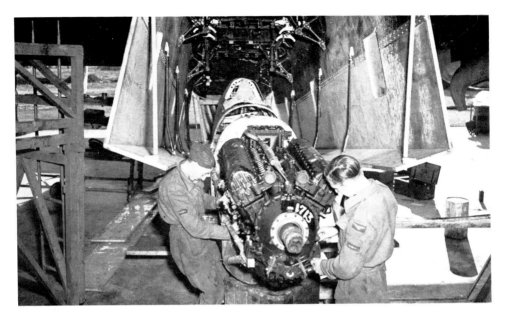

R.A.F. mechanics in North Africa work on a Spitfire's engine beneath the bomb-bay of a Halifax converted for the purpose of carrying a Spitfire fuselage.

[*I.W.M.*

Wellington 'L-for-London' is refuelled among the cacti at an airfield in Algeria. Mainstay of No. 205 Group in the Middle East, the faithful Wimpey continued to play a significant part in the Group's offensive until 1944, by which time operations were being conducted from Italy. [*I.W.M.*

Ground crews prepare a Blenheim V, or 'Bisley' as the type was known in the R.A.F., for operations at an airfield in Algeria. Four R.A.F. squadrons flew Bisleys in North Africa and the C.O. of No. 18 (Bisley) Squadron, Wing Cdr. H. G. Malcolm, earned a posthumous V.C. for a highly-gallant operation against an enemy airfield at Chouigui on December 12, 1942.

[I.W.M.

A flight of Boston light bombers takes off from a desert landing ground to join its escort, already waiting overhead. If the target was a vital one, the bombers would probably attack it a second and even a third time, maintaining a 'shuttle service' throughout the day.

[I.W.M.

Spitfires and Hurricanes undergoing repair at a North African depot in 1943. [*I.W.M.*

Spitfires fly over columns of American troops during the Allied victory parade in Tunis on May 20, 1943. All the Allied commanders were present and the salute at the march-past was taken by Generals Eisenhower, Alexander, Anderson and Giraud.

[*I.W.M.*

Two great leaders in the Middle East. Air Chief Marshal Sir Arthur Tedder, A.O.C.-in-C. Middle East, and (right) Air Vice Marshal (later Air Marshal) Sir Arthur 'Mary' Coningham, A.O.C.-in-C. Western Desert, at Advanced Air Headquarters in the desert.   [*I.W.M.*

Wellington XIII of No. 8 Squadron, Aden. During the war general-reconnaissance aircraft operating from Aden were responsible for the protection of Allied shipping over an area which included not only the Gulf of Aden but, eventually, the Persian Gulf also. In April 1944 alone, they flew well over 2,000 hours and, although nothing of note happened, the crews of the Aden-based squadrons safely escorted 2,000,000 tons of shipping through their areas.

R.A.F. ground crews service a Baltimore in a stone blast bay on an airfield near one of Malta's most-bombed towns in 1943. [*I.W.M.*

Bombs being loaded into a Halifax of No. 462 (R.A.A.F.) Squadron in Libya *circa* December 1943. This unit made nightly raids on the Germans in Greece, Dodecanese Islands and Sicily, and claimed to have been the last squadron to bomb Sicily before the historic Allied landing. [*I.W.M.*

Wintry scene on an airfield in the Midlands occupied by an R.C.A.F. Hampden bomber unit—No. 408 'Goose' Squadron. This squadron was the last in Bomber Command to use Hampdens operationally, the final mission being an attack against Wilhelmshaven on the night of September 14-15, 1942.

[*I.W.M.*

Down in the dump. Armourers, working in wintry conditions, roll out bombs ready for loading on to trolleys which will transport them to the waiting Halifaxes at a bomber station in Yorkshire.

[*I.W.M.*

Above: Cockpit of a Short Stirling bomber.
[*Aeroplane*

Right: Navigator in a Stirling. [*I.W.M.*

EUROPE

1942 to D-Day

W.A.A.F. transport driver watches a bomber crew of No. 115 (Wellington) Squadron disembark from the vehicle she has driven to the dispersal point at Marham, Norfolk, *circa* June 1942.

Right: Avro Lancaster Is of No. 207 Squadron, Bottesford, Leicestershire, in vic formation over the English countryside in about June 1942. The 'Lanc' was the finest heavy bomber used by the R.A.F. in World War II and, in all, flew 156,192 operational sorties with Bomber Command. It dropped 608,612 tons of bombs and a large, but unknown, tonnage of mines. By March 1945 no fewer than 56 squadrons of Bomber Command were equipped with Lancasters.   [*Charles E. Brown*

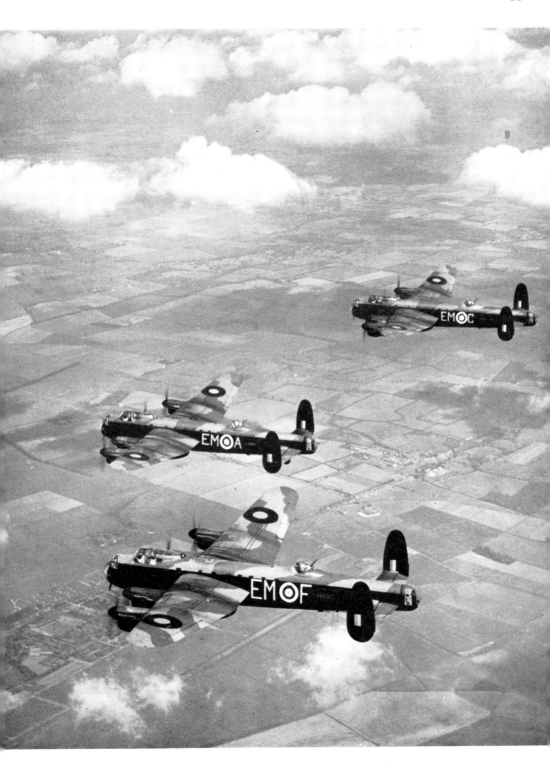

Wireless operator of a Lancaster. [*I.W.M.*

W.A.A.F. electrician makes adjustments to the bomb release gear of a Lancaster. [*I.W.M.*

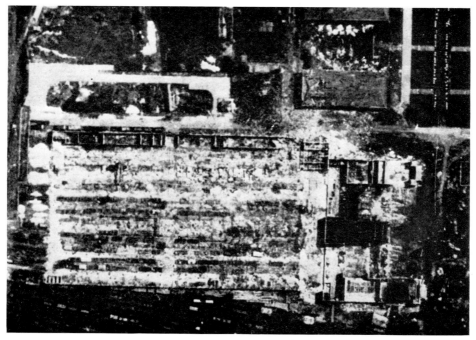

Factory at Deutz on the east bank of the Rhine before and after the 1,000-bomber raid on Cologne in May 1942. *[I.W.M.*

The A.T.C. lends a hand. Many hundreds of Air Training Corps cadets spent their wartime holidays on R.A.F. airfields in Britain where they helped the 'regulars'—and if they were lucky got a 'flip' during an air-test as their reward. A.T.C. boys pull a trolley load of incendiary bomb containers to a Stirling bomber of No. 15 Squadron at Wyton, Hunts., in readiness for the night's raid, early in August 1942. 'Last night aircraft of Bomber Command laid mines in enemy waters' Behind that familiar terse phrase in R.A.F. communiques there was a story of brilliant planning and flying by our pilots under extremely hazardous conditions.

This picture (left) shows ground staff loading mines, or 'vegetables' as they were code-named into a Lancaster of No. 106 Squadron at Syerston, Notts., in November 1942. This particular Lanc was captained by the late Wing Cdr. J. de J. Wooldridge who later commanded No. 105 Squadron—one of the two Mosquito squadrons whose work he describes in his well-known book Low Attack. In the background of our photo can be seen one of No. 106 Squadron's abandoned Manchesters.

'O.K. chaps, any questions?' Boston crews of No. 88 Squadron in No. 2 Group are briefed by the C.O. before take-off. [*I.W.M.*

Douglas Boston IIIs of No. 107 Squadron photographed from the C.O.'s machine in 1942. This American-built light bomber equipped four home-based R.A.F. bomber squadrons, plus two R.A.F. intruder squadrons, and did good work on daylight raids against Continental fringe targets. It was faster than the Blenheim IV, which it supplanted, and was far more popular with the No. 2 Group crews.
[*Flight International*

Bostons over the target during the big daylight raid on the Philips radio and valve works at Eindhoven, Holland, on December 6, 1942. Ninety-three aircraft of No. 2 Group took part in this operation and, although severe damage was done to the factory, 15 bombers were lost (16 per cent of the force) and another 53 were damaged. [*I.W.M.*

de Havilland Mosquito B.IV of No. 105 Squadron, based at Marham, Norfolk, in December 1942. The 'Mossie' was used in numerous roles but is, perhaps, best remembered for its precision day bombing with No. 2 Group (and, later, 2nd T.A.F.) and its night pathfinding and nuisance raiding with Nos. 5 and 8 Groups. It was so fast that it was rarely intercepted by enemy fighters and it enjoyed the lowest loss rate of any aircraft with Bomber Command.

[*Aeroplane*

Whitley G.R.VII of No. 612 Squadron festooned with Air-to-Surface Vessel (ASV) radar aerials. The Whitley VII entered Coastal Command service at the end of 1941 and, on November 30, one such machine of No. 502 Squadron from Chivenor, Devon, made the first A.S.V. 'kill' by sinking *U-206* in the Bay of Biscay. Whitleys remained in squadron service with Coastal Command until early 1943. *[Aeroplane*

R.A.F. officers examine a visiting Cierva C-30 Rota autogyro at a Coastal Command airfield in 1942. During the war the Rotas were used for radar calibration and operated as independent units with a pilot, engine fitter and rigger. These units moved around the coastal radar stations, and the aircraft flew out to sea to send back signals to be picked up by the radar stations. On arrival at the series of pre-arranged points the Rota dropped a sea-marker and orbited it at a known height. Visible in the background of the photograph is a Whitley V of No. 612 Squadron equipped with ASV radar. *[I.W.M.*

Kit inspection for
the crew of a Cata
lina of Coasta
Command stat
ioned at Gibralta
From Gib the Ca
crews, together with
their comrades who
flew Sunderlands
set out to search
far and wide over
the Atlantic and
Mediterranean for
lurking U-boats.

[*I.W.M.*

Depth charges are
loaded on to the
underwing racks
of a Sunderlan
flying-boat at a
base in West Africa
Sunderlands firs
operated from Wes
Africa in March
1941 in order to
extend their activi
ties to the South
Atlantic.   [*I.W.M.*

ght photograph taken
a Sunderland during
attack on a U-boat.
e three large balls of
ht are flares dropped by
e Sunderland to illu-
nate the U-boat before
e attack. The outline of
e enemy submarine can
seen in the swirling
am. [*I.W.M.*

picture which speaks
r itself. The Spitfire
own was responsible
r 15 of its squadron's
ills'.

North American Mustang I of No. 2 Squadron 'beats up' its home airfield at Sawbridgeworth, Essex, in July 1942. This famous American-built type was conceived originally in 1940 to British specifications and only afterwards was it taken into service with the U.S.A.A.F. Early marks of R.A.F. Mustangs had Allison engines and, because they were handicapped at high altitudes by a lack of power, were used for armed tactical reconnaissance instead of normal fighter duties. They supplanted the Tomahawks in squadrons of Army Co-operation Command and in October 1942 became the first R.A.F. single-engined fighters to fly over Germany, in a raid on the Dortmund-Ems Canal.
[*Aeroplane*

Hawker Typhoon roars overhead displaying its black and white stripes, the purpose of which was to avoid confusion with the *Luftwaffe's* Focke-Wulf 190. Armed with bombs or rockets, plus its four cannon, the 'Tiffy', in its cross-Channel sweeps, destroyed everything from locomotives to radar stations and later helped to clear the way for the Allied armies during their advance through France and Holland.

One of the high-speed launches of the R.A.F. 'Navy' which went to the rescue of both Allied and enemy aircrew brought down in the sea. The Air-Sea Rescue Service, as it was properly known, began as an improvisation during the Battle of Britain. By the end of the war its total 'catch' included 3,723 R.A.F. and 1,998 American airmen rescued from the waters around the shores of Britain, and at least 3,200 aircrew and 4,665 soldiers, sailors and civilians rescued overseas.   [*I.W M.*

Among the various types of aircraft used by the Air-Sea Rescue Service was the Supermarine Walrus, or 'Shagbat' as it was affectionately known. Usually, the Walrus did the actual rescue work after the Lysanders had spotted downed airmen in their dinghies. Picture shows a Shagbat battling through the choppy sea to pick up a 'survivor' during a training exercise.

Time off for a cuppa. Two Canadian pilots of Hawker Hector glider tugs take a welcome break for tea at a Y.M.C.A. tea car, which stands alongside a General Aircraft Hotspur training glider at an airfield 'somewhere in Britain'. Y.M.C.A. tea cars, like their N.A.A.F.I. counterparts, were a familiar feature of home airfields during the war and—to use that well-worn phrase—they did a wonderful job.

Winston Churchill in the cockpit of the famous R.A.F. Liberator V.I.P. transport *Commando* on the occasion of his visit to Turkey in April 1943. Note the Red Star and hammer and sickle insignia, denoting a previous trip to Russia.

[*I.W.M.*

One of the lesser-known types used by Transport Command during the war was the Wellington C.XVI. This was a conversion from the Mk.IC bomber, with gun turrets removed, bomb bay sealed, seats fitted in the fuselage and —as in the case of the No. 24 Squadron example illustrated—dummy turrets to camouflage its defencelessness. Similar conversions from the Wellingtons I and IA were designated C.I and C.XV.

Cloak and dagger Lizzie. During the war several R.A.F. squadrons, both at home and overseas, were engaged on clandestine operations involving the landing or picking up of Allied secret agents, or 'Joes' as they were known, in enemy territory. Two U.K.-based squadrons which performed this extremely hazardous work were Nos. 138 and 166 Squadrons, based at Tempsford, Beds. The most-used type of machine for landings and pick-ups was the ubiquitous Lysander, and an example of the Mk. 5 Special Duties version—painted black and fitted with a ladder and a long-range fuel tank—is pictured below.

In World War II—as was also the case in 1914-18—the British aircraft industry rose magnificently to the task of providing the R.A.F. with vast quantities of high-quality weapons. It employed a peak of 1,800,000 people, of whom about 40 per cent were women, and turned out a total of 124,109 aircraft and well over a quarter of a million engines. Here Avro Lancasters are seen during final assembly at Armstrong Whitworth's factory at Coventry—one of several major centres of wartime Lancaster production.

Responsible for delivery to the R.A.F. of the bulk of the Industry's output of new aeroplanes, and also the American types which arrived in England, was the Air Transport Auxiliary. This organisation started with 30 amateur pilots and finally totalled over 700 men and women who, between 1939 and 1945, ferried more than 308,000 aircraft of more than 100 different types from the factories to the R.A.F. With a few exceptions the A.T.A. pilots flew entirely without the aid of wireless, and in almost any weather, and during the war years it was safe to assume that every British aircraft seen in the sky had been or would be flown at some period of its life by one of their number. Picture shows pilots of a Ferry Pool setting off in a taxi Anson for the day's work. *[Aeroplane*

Fortress IIA sets out on an Atlantic patrol. Machines of this type, operating from bases in south-west England, the Hebrides, Iceland and the Azores, together with Liberators, greatly diminished the area in which German U-boats were free from the attention of our air forces and were responsible for many U-boat 'kills' in the Atlantic.　　[*I.W.M.*

Liberator G.R.III in flight. In Coastal Command service the Lib was employed mainly as a very-long-range (V.L.R.) aircraft with extra fuel tanks and certain equipment removed. Many examples were fitted with A.S.V. radar and Leigh Lights. One Liberator pilot, F/O L. A. Trigg, R.N.Z.A.F., won a posthumous Victoria Cross for his gallantry in pressing home an attack on a U-boat, which he destroyed before his machine crashed into the sea.

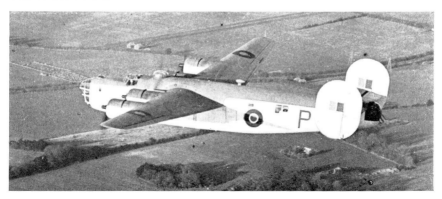

Above: Coastal Command Liberator G.R.III illuminated by the beam of another Liberator's Leigh Light during a test. The Leigh Light was a powerful searchlight fitted to Coastal Command aircraft engaged in hunting U-boats at night. It threw a flat but broad beam for a considerable distance and enabled the aircraft to press home its attack. It was introduced in June 1942; by August the U-boats were afraid to surface at night, and came up during the day, providing possible visible targets.　　　[*I.W.M.*

Opposite, top: Lockheed Venturas of No. 21 Squadron on a flight from Methwold, Norfolk, in January 1943. Known as 'the Flying Pig' because of its porcine fuselage, the Ventura was used by three squadrons of No. 2 Group for daylight bombing but was not a success as it was no match for enemy fighters. It was withdrawn from Bomber Command in late 1943 but subsequently did useful work with Coastal Command, mainly in the meteorological reconnaissance role.　　　[*Aeroplane*

Opposite, bottom: North American Mitchell IIs of No. 180 Squadron, at Foulsham, Norfolk, in July 1943. These light day bombers began operations with No. 2 Group in January 1943 and served eventually with six squadrons of 2 Group and 2nd T.A.F. In the closing months of the war some of them operated from Continental bases. [*Aeroplane*

Below: From the palace in 'hansom' style. F/O Colin Steley, an R.A.A.F. Sunderland flying-boat captain from Ayr, Queensland, leaves Buckingham Palace in a hansom cab after receiving the D.F.C. at an investiture in June 1943.

Left: Many Halifa
bombers serve
with Coastal Com
mand from la
1942 onwards
the meteorologic
reconnaissance ar
anti-shipping role
Favourite huntin
grounds were th
Bay of Biscay an
fjords off the No
wegian coast and
the Skagerrak an
Kattegat—an
many blockade rur
ners and U-boa
became their vic
tims.   Here th
crew of a white
painted Halifa
G.R.II Series
make a last chec
of the route befo
taking off fro
Stornoway.
                [*I.W.M.*

Right: 'Bombe
Harris,   AOC-in-
Bomber Comman
from 1942 to 194
chatting with A
Cdre. G. A. Walk
(now Air Marsh
Sir Augustus Wa
ker) during a visit t
the Halifax bomb
station at Pocklinç
ton, Yorks, on Ma
10, 1943.   I
December 194
while commandin
R.A.F.   Syersto
Notts, 'Gus' Walk
lost his right ar
when a blazing Lar
caster exploded a
he was attemptin
to rescue its crev
Also seen in th
photo is Air Vice
Marshal C. R. Ca
(later Air Marsha
Sir Roderick Carr
AOC-in-C No.
Bomber Group.

As dusk gathers, a Halifax II Srs.I (Special) of No. 102 Squadron at Pockling-
ton, Yorks., gets the take-off signal on the night of June 19/20, 1943, when
the target was the Schneider armament works at Le Creusot, France. The
black-and-white checked vehicle at the left of the picture is the airfield
controller's caravan.   [I.W.M.

Lancaster I 'O-for-Orange' of No. 207 Squadron on display in Trafalgar
Square during London's 'Wings for Victory Week' in March 1943. [Aeroplane

Wg. Cdr. Guy Gibson's Lancaster of No. 617 Squadron carrying one of Sir Barnes Wallis's remarkable bouncing bombs of the type used to breach the Ruhr dams in May 1943.

The Möhne dam breached after the attack by No. 617 Squadron. Note the balloon barrage. The epic raid of May 16-17, 1943, on this and other Ruhr dams has been described officially as 'a feat of arms which has never been excelled'. Of the 19 Lancasters which took off for the raid, with their 133 men, eight did not return.

Halifax of No. 158 Squadron that landed back at its base at Lissett, Yorks., after attacking Cologne on the night of June 28, 1943, with a hole in the fuselage measuring 5ft by 4ft. [*I.W.M.*

Panic spreader. Two 500-lb bombs being loaded on to a Typhoon in June 1943. The Tiffy's bomb load was originally 500lb, but advanced to 1,000lb and then to 2,000lb. It was the only R.A.F. fighter-bomber capable of carrying such a load.

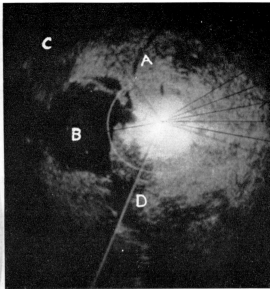

Bomber Command's 'magic eye'. Area south-west of Swinemunde on the Baltic coast displayed on the screen of an H2S set inside a bomber. Note, by comparison with map, how land shows up lighter than water. [*I.W.M.*

Members of No. 75 (New Zealand) Squadron with one of their Stirlings. This R.N.Z.A.F. squadron was formed in April 1940 as a Wellington unit and in the closing months of the war flew Lancasters, having flown Stirlings in the period between.

A 12,000-lb high-capacity bomb parked in front of a Lancaster of No. 57 Squadron. This type of bomb was made up of three main sections, plus the tail, and was first used operationally on the night of September 15/16, 1943, by Lancasters of No. 617 in a disastrous low-level attack on the Dortmund-Ems canal (five out of eight aircraft were lost).   [*I.W.M.*

Mail time at an R.C.A.F. Wellington bomber station in Yorkshire. The first Canadian squadron in Bomber Command was formed in April 1941 and eventually Canada contributed an entire Group—No. 6 Group. At the war's end 6 Group comprised 14 squadrons flying Halifaxes and Lancasters, some of the latter being Canadian-built Mk.Xs. From 1942 the original R.C.A.F. heavy bomber squadron served with No. 8 Group—the Pathfinder Force.

Fido, Fido burning bright . . . Many valuable aircraft and lives were saved in World War II by this striking device, *Fido* (Fog Investigation and Dispersal Operation). It consisted of petrol burners installed at short intervals along the principal runway of selected U.K. airfields and, when lit, heated the air to disperse fog sufficiently for the aircraft to land. *Fido* was installed at three main airfields—Carnaby (Yorkshire), Manston (Kent) and Woodbridge (Suffolk)—plus twelve others between 1942 and VE-Day and, altogether, 2,524 landings and 182 take-offs were made with *Fido* during the war. Picture shows a Lancaster taking off with the aid of *Fido*.   [*I.W.M.*

Lancaster (bottom left) silhouetted against the glow of thousands of incendiary bombs and fires burning in the area south-south-east of Hanover's main railway station, during an attack by 430 aircraft of Bomber Command on the night of October 8-9, 1943. So clearly are many of the main streets picked out in this great saturation of fire that exact identification of the locality presented no problem to the photographic interpreters. The broad white 'ribbon' running from the bottom left—just under the nose of the aircraft—to the top right corner, is the Salle Strasse. In this attack two square miles of the city centre were devastated.   [*I.W.M.*

Above: Air gunner of a British bomber which was shot down in the suburbs of Berlin being interrogated by the Germans. [*I.W.M.*

Opposite, top: Lancaster at dispersal, ready to take off for Berlin on the night of January 2-3, 1944. Bombs painted on its nose signify that it has already made 71 operational sorties. [*I.W.M.*

Opposite, bottom: Crews of an Australian Halifax bomber squadron being interrogated on their return from a raid over Berlin in January 1944. Left to right: F/Sgt. G. P. Tomlins of Hastings, N.Z. (the only Maori in the squadron), F/Sgt. R. J. Harding of Sydney, N.S.W., F/Sgt. E. Schuman of Brisbane, Queensland (Captain), F/Lt. R. D. King-Scott of Perth, Western Australia (Gunnery Officer), and Sqn. Ldr. R. Crawley (R.A.F. Intelligence Officer).

Some of the aircraft used by the Empire Central Flying School during the war. Front line, from right: Mosquito, Typhoon, Spitfire, Proctor, Tarpon, Hurricane, Masters (3). Back line: Anson, Oxford, Tiger Moth, Lancaster, Magister, Wellington, Havoc, Mitchell, Master, Stirling. In the foreground is a Hotspur glider.

Mosquito F.B.VI tests its four 20-mm cannon and four 0.303-in machine-guns. Carrying also two 500-lb bombs, or sometimes eight rocket projectiles, the fighter-bomber Mossies operated round-the-clock in virtually all weathers and there were many nights after D-Day when they were the only Allied aircraft active.

An armourer loads rocket projectiles on to the wing racks of a Mosquito F.B.VI.

Mosquito F.B.VI of Coastal Command attacks a U-boat with rocket projectiles.   [I.W.M.

Armourers belt up cannon ammunition at a 2nd T.A.F. station in Britain.
In the background are some Spitfire IXs, including aircraft of Nos. 56 and 332
Squadrons.   [*I.W.M.*

Cockpit of a Mosquito night fighter showing the A.I. radar receiver. The
screen is fitted with a vizor.   [*I.W.M.*

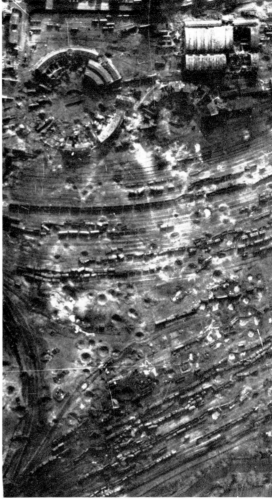

The breach in the south side of the outer wall of Amiens gaol following the famous daylight precision attack by Mosquitos of No. 2 Group on February 18, 1944. The gaol contained over 700 prisoners, including well over 100 loyal Frenchmen awaiting execution for their efforts in helping the Allied cause. As a result of the Mosquito attack, 258 prisoners escaped, including over half the doomed patriots; but the bombs killed 102, of whom many were not political prisoners. Moreover, many of those who made their escape that day were subsequently recaptured.

[*I.W.M.*

Between April and June 1944 R.A.F. Bomber Command and the U.S.A.A.F. mounted a heavy pre-invasion bombing offensive against key railway centres in France and Belgium—the so-called 'Transportation Plan'. Here is the rail centre at Amiens after a pinpoint attack by the R.A.F. Scores of craters overlap where the tracks once ran; two engine roundhouses (top) are almost completely destroyed, and there is severe damage to a locomotive shed (top right). Rolling stock has suffered heavily.   [*I.W.M.*

SICILY — ITALY

R.A.F. temporary flight office sheltered from the sun beneath the wing of a German Storch aircraft on Comiso airfield in Sicily.

[*I.W.M.*

R.A.F. Servicing Commandos go out to service a Spitfire on the newly-captured airfield at Comiso in Sicily in August 1943. [*I.W.M.*

R.A.F. padre conducts a religious service at an airfield in Sicily. [*I.W.M.*

A large tent on an Italian farm serves as the Orderly Room of an R.A.F. Wing
Headquarters in Italy.   [*I.W.M.*

Spitfire is manhandled to free it from the mud on a waterlogged landing
ground in Italy.   [*I.W.M.*

Spitfire pilots at a landing strip in the Anzio beach-head, Italy, 'scramble' from a dug-out. Left to right are Capt. R. Taylor, S.A.A.F., of Johannesburg, F/O C. Turcott of Ontario, Canada, and Lt. A. Cawood of Louis-Trichardt, South Africa. [*I.W.M.*

Fairchild Argus used for 'spotting' takes off from a narrow Italian beach in 1944. Also in the picture are a Fieseler Storch (ex-*Luftwaffe*) and a Vultee Vigilant. [*I.W.M.*

Above: R.A.F. Dakotas, which were employed on dropping supplies by parachute to Balkan partisans, lined up at an airfield in Italy. The transport squadrons' supply and special duty missions —the latter usually flown at night over difficult mountainous country and all too often in appalling weather—were a major factor in the success achieved by those who fought so stubbornly behind the Italian front. By the end of the war, Allied aircraft had flown some 11,600 sorties to Yugoslavia alone, to drop, or land at specially-built airstrips, over 16,400 tons of supplies. In 'pick-up' operations, some 2,500 persons were flown into that country and over 19,000, mostly wounded, brought out.   [*I.W.M.*

Right: Martin Marauder of No. 39 Squadron of the Desert Air Force bombs a railway bridge over the river Asino at Chiaravalle, near the Adriatic coast in Italy. Two R.A.F. squadrons flew the Marauder—Nos. 14 and 39—No. 14 being mainly employed in a maritime reconnaissance role while No. 39 was a normal day-bomber unit.   [*I.W.M.*

Below: Baltimore 'R-for-Redwing' taxies out for take-off on a night sortie at an airfield in Italy. On its nose are recorded 80 operations, 66 of them night sorties.   [*I.W.M.*

Above: Enemy rail wagons and oil tanks piled on top of each other near Arezzo, Italy, on a wrecked railway line.   [*I.W.M.*

Right: The Liberator became the main strategic bomber of the R.A.F. in Italy, just as it also did in S.E.A.C., in both cases replacing the Wellington. This one, V-Victor of No. 37 Squadron, was hit by two bombs from another aircraft flying above it during a raid on Monfalcone, Italy, on March 16, 1945. The bombs had not fallen far enough to become live and explode, but the port inner propeller was knocked off, a gaping hole made in the fuselage and the dorsal turret wrecked. Fortunately there were no casualties among the crew and the crippled Lib managed to fly over 300 miles back to base and land safely.   [*I.W.M.*

Below: Wellington Xs of No. 205 Group on an airfield of the Foggia group, in Italy, ready to take off on a night bombing mission. The last of No. 205 Group's Wimpys were replaced by Liberators in March 1945.   [*I.W.M.*

Douglas Bostons of No. 88 Squadron, 2nd T.A.F., marked with invasion stripes, prepare for smokescreen-laying sorties over the Normandy beaches in June 1944.

[*I.W.M.*

EUROPE from D-Day

Men of the Airborne Regiment read slogans chalked on their Airspeed Horsa glider before taking off for Normandy on the evening of D-Day (June 6, 1944) to reinforce Allied troops landed there some hours previously.   [*I.W.M.*

Part of the force of 250 R.A.F. gliders and their tugs which flew to the Caen area of Northern France on the evening of D-Day in the largest main glider assault that had been made so far. Vessels of the Allied invasion fleet lie close to the French shore, where fires can be seen burning on the beaches. *[I.W.M.*

Supplies are dropped by parachute from Stirlings in answer to a radioed request by men of one of our Airborne divisions in Normandy in June 1944. *[I.W.M.*

One of the immediate tasks of the Allies during the Normandy landings was to establish airstrips just behind the front line. It was the job of R.A.F. Servicing Commandos to be on the spot as the first R.A.F. aircraft arrived and to provide full ground service. Here, some of these men, at a 2nd T.A.F. Mustang strip, enjoy a game of cards during a break.   [*I.W.M.*

Spitfire taxies past a Typhoon at an airstrip in France on its return from a sortie over enemy lines in the summer of 1944. Owing to the clouds of dust stirred up by the aircraft, the men of this Spitfire squadron dubbed themselves the 'Dust Rats'.   [*I.W.M.*

The lives of many Allied soldiers wounded in Normandy were saved by rapid transportation by air to hospitals in England. W.A.A.F. nursing orderlies attended to the wounded on airfields in France and within a few hours they were in a British hospital. Photo shows wounded men being transferred from an ambulance to a waiting Dakota on an airfield in Normandy in June 1944.

[*I.W.M.*

Flying control at work on an R.A.F. airstrip in France, 1944.   *W.M.*

Booze wagon.   Beer is transferred from kegs to a converted fuel tank for
delivery by Spitfire to the R.A.F. in Normandy.   [*I.W.M.*

Mosquito reconnaissance aircraft prepares to take off to check enemy troop
movements in Germany.   [*I.W.M.*

Left: Introduction of the gyro gunsight during the later part of the war greatly increased the accuracy of shooting, even by average pilots, and it is no exaggeration to say that it doubled the efficiency of R.A.F. fighter aircraft. This ingenious electrical mechanism provided the pilot automatically with the correct target at which to aim as soon as he had made two simple adjustments, and thus largely eliminated the possibility of human error. In our picture the pilot is adjusting the dial, on which are marked the settings for different types of enemy aircraft. [*I.W.M.*

Below: Death of a U-boat. Action photograph, taken by a Sunderland of No. 10 (R.A.A.F.) Squadron, Coastal Command, just as its depth charges exploded beneath the *U*-243, 130 miles southwest of Brest on July 8, 1944. A track of machine-gun fire from the Sunderland's rear turret can be seen leading across the water to the U-boat. This fire killed the U-boat's captain and coxwain. After the attack, the U-boat began to sink, and another Sunderland and a Liberator later attacked it, to make its destruction certain. [*I.W.M.*

Above: Wg Cdr. J. E. 'Johnny' Johnson, top-scoring R.A.F. fighter pilot of World War II, on the wing of his Spitfire with his Labrador retriever, Sally. Picture was taken during a break between operations on an airfield in France, where he commanded a Canadian Spitfire Wing.   [*I.W.M.*

Right: Destruction caused by R.A.F. Bomber Command to Volkel airfield, 12 miles north of Helmond, Holland, on September 3, 1944. This photograph was one of several taken by a Photographic Reconnaissance Unit aircraft and the whole set showed 800 craters on the airfield, in addition to damage to buildings.   [*I.W.M.*

The devastated town of Darmstadt, important centre of the German chemical industry and a trunk railway junction, after Bomber Command's attack of September 11/12, 1944. [*I.W.M.*

Paratroop element of the British 1st Airborne Division lands at Arnhem, Holland, on September 17, 1944. [*I.W.M.*

Right: A photograph taken to the east of Boulogne on the morning of September 17, 1944, during Army support operations by Nos. 5 and 8 Groups. It shows the concentration of bomb bursts and target indicators, with a Lancaster of No. 61 Squadron overhead.

Below: Lancasters of Bomber Command return from an attack on German targets in the Pas de Calais in the summer of 1944.
[*I.W.M.*

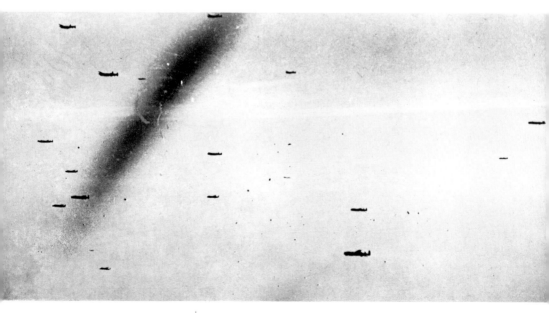

A 12,000-lb deep-penetration bomb, or *Tallboy*. These huge bombs, like their even bigger successors, the 22,000-lb *Grand Slams*, were designed by Sir Barnes Wallis of Vickers-Armstrongs. They were highly streamlined and had their fins offset so that they spun as they dropped, the gyroscopic action holding them perfectly steady as they plunged through the sonic barrier. Both bombs were carried exclusively by Lancasters, the *Tallboy* being introduced operationally by No. 617 Squadron in a raid on the Saumur railway tunnel on the night of June 8-9, 1944. [*I.W.M.*

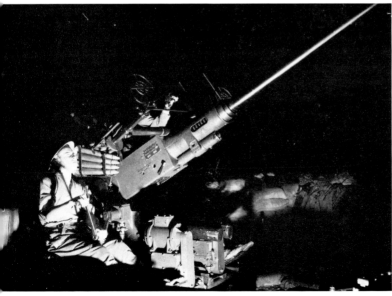

R.A.F. Regiment fights the flying bomb. A crew is illuminated by the gun flash. [*I.W.M.*

Remarkable photograph taken by a P.R. Mosquito showing damage caused in two attacks by Bomber Command 'heavies' on a German V-weapon site at Wizernes, in the Pas de Calais, in July 1944. The complex concrete structure, comprising numerous tunnels pointing towards London and topped by a massive dome, was built at the edge of a chalk quarry. In the first attack, made by Lancasters of No. 617 Squadron, on July 17, two and possibly three 12,000-lb *Tallboy* earthquake bombs burst right on the target, causing most of the damage seen in the photo. In the second attack, on July 20, the ground all around the quarry was ploughed up by ordinary bombs and masses of constructional machinery were wrecked.   [*I.W.M.*

Right: Spitfire moves through a gap in the clouds to knock out a V-1 flying bomb bound for England. Sometimes, instead of shooting them down, our fighter pilots flew alongside the 'buzz bombs' and tipped them over with a wing-tip, which made them crash out of control. [*I.W.M.*

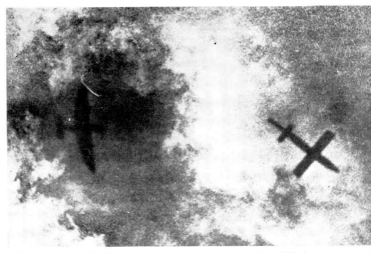

Below: More buzz-bomb killers: Hawker Tempest Vs of No. 501 Squadron, Hawkinge, Kent. Developed from the Typhoon, the Tempest entered service in April 1944 when the first Tempest Wing, led by Wg Cdr. Roland Beamont, was formed at Newchurch, and it destroyed 638 V-1s out of the R.A.F.'s total of 1,771 between June 13 and September 5. Tempests served later with equal distinction on the Continent, in support of advancing Allied ground forces, and by VE-Day had destroyed 20 Me 262 jets in air combat. [*Charles E. Brown*

Female worker puts the finishing touches to a Napier Sabre engine—powerplant of the Tempest V—on the assembly line.

Marshal of the R.A.F. Lord Trenchard talks to Sqn. Ldr. D. H. Smith, from South Australia, and pilots of No. 453 R.A.A.F. fighter squadron during a visit to liberated France. The airmen had just returned from an armed reconnaissance, during which they wrecked 22 enemy motor transports.   [*I.W.M.*

Right: Crews of Bomber Command's Meteorological Flight Mosquitos flew in all kinds of weather to gain vital information about met. conditions in enemy territory and so enable reliable forecasts to be made for the benefit of the 'bomber boys'. Here L.A.C. Bennett of Bow, London, paints the 161st sortie mark on veteran Met. Flight Mosquito 'D-for-Dorothy'.

[*I.W.M.*

Below: When Allied troops occupied this airfield between Versailles and Chateaufort, France, in the autumn of 1944, they found captured Spitfires, Hurricanes and U.S.A.A.F. p-47s, which the Germans had been repairing; they were wrecked by the Germans before their withdrawal.

A Mitchell flies over the target during an attack by aircraft of the 2nd T.A.F. on a rail bridge at Deventer, eight miles north of Zutphen, Holland, in the autumn of 1944.   *[I.W.M.*

Beaufighters set fire to a tanker in the Skagerrak on October 15, 1944. Two of the attacking Beaus sweep low over the stricken vessel as a column of smoke rises from it.   *[I.W.M.*

German Battleship *Tirpitz* lies capsized in Trömso fjord, Norway, after the famous daylight attack by Lancasters of Nos. 9 and 617 Squadrons, armed with 12,000-lb *Tallboy* streamlined bombs and led by Wg Cdr. J. B. 'Willy' Tait on November 12, 1944. The attack—the third to be made in the latter part of 1944—was executed from between 12,850 and 16,000 feet, and two Lancasters scored direct hits with their *Tallboys*.   [*I.W.M.*

Black-painted Fortresses of Nos. 214 and 223 Squadrons of No. 100 Group, fitted with powerful radio and radar-jamming devices with code-names like *Jostle, Mandrel, Tinsel* and *Piperack*, played havoc with the *Luftwaffe's* early warning and fighter-control systems in the closing stages of the war. In so doing, they greatly reduced the casualty rate of the main force heavies of Bomber Command. Other specially-equipped machines which took part in Bomber Command's secret war in the ether included Halifaxes, Lancasters, Stirlings, Liberators and Mosquitos.

Crew of a Free French Air Force Halifax bomber study their route to the target before taking off on a daylight raid from Elvington, Yorks, in 1944; in the French bomber squadrons it was the bomb-aimer who was captain of the aircraft and not the pilot, as is usual in other air forces.

Many Bomber Command Lancasters flew more than 100 operations, but the one with the greatest number of ops to its credit was this Mk.I, ED888 'M2', or 'Mike Squared', of Nos. 103 and 576 Squadrons. It was withdrawn from active service in January 1945 on completion of 140 sorties, including 98 to Germany (15 of them to Berlin). In our photo 'Mike Squared' is being awarded a bar to its D.F.C. by Grp. Capt. W. S. Sheen, O.C. R.A.F. Elsham Wolds, Lincs, on completion of its 131st operational sortie in November 1944.

Christmas cracker for the Führer. Armourers push a 4,000-lb high-capacity bomb, or 'cookie', towards the gaping bomb bay of a Mosquito B.XVI of No. 128 Pathfinder Squadron at Warboys, Hunts, at Christmas 1944. The fast, high-flying Mossies of No. 8 Group's Light Night Striking Force used to drop their cookies on Berlin and other German cities and, as often as not, were on their way home before the enemy fighters were alerted. Their nuisance raids undoubtedly had a considerable effect on the enemy's morale and kept him guessing as to where the bombers were likely to strike next.

A Christmas tree lends a touch of homely atmosphere during the service held in York Minster, and attended by over 1,000 men and women of the R.C.A.F., to mark the second anniversary of the Canadian Bomber Group which formed on New Year's Day 1943. Centuries-old stone figures look on in silence as the band plays a hymn.

Above: Spitfire fighter-bombers, each loaded with one 500-lb and two 250-lb bombs, wait to take off from an advanced airfield in Holland to harrass enemy communications in late 1944. [*I.W.M.*

Opposite, top: An airborne lifeboat of the type carried by Vickers Warwick aircraft during air-sea rescue operations from mid-1943 onward. The 27-ft boat, made of wood with two buoyancy chambers, had two engines, sails, food and wireless, was self-righting and could be dropped by parachute to save airmen adrift in the sea out of reach of rescue launches. Airborne lifeboats were first carried by Hudson aircraft of the Air-Sea Rescue Service.

Opposite, bottom: Spitfire P.R. XI in the snow on an R.A.F. airfield in Holland, photographed through a roll of landing strip wire. [*I.W.M.*

Above: Gloster Meteor IIIs of No. 616 Squadron, 2nd T.A.F., take off from Nijmegen airfield near Brussels, during the closing weeks of the war. No. 616 Squadron, in July 1944, at Culmhead, became the first R.A.F. squadron to receive jet aircraft (Meteor Is) and, following a move to Manston, first took them into action on the 27th of that month against the flying-bombs. The first 'kill' was scored on August 4, near Tonbridge, by F/O T. D. Dean in EE216. [*Charles E. Brown*

Above: The railway viaduct at Bielefeld which carried the main line from Hamm to Hanover, photographed on March 17, 1945, after the famous attack by Lancasters of No. 617 Squadron—the 'Dam Busters'—three days earlier, with 22,000-lb and 12,000-lb bombs, and previous attacks by U.S. heavy bombers. The huge size of the craters can be seen when compared with the house in the foreground. Since the war, the viaduct has been by-passed by a loopline, but the wrecked structure itself remains to this day as a monument to the destructive power of Bomber Command.
[*I.W.M.*

Below: This large blackboard on the wall opposite the C-in-C's desk in the Ops Room at Bomber Command H.Q. presented a daily picture of the Command's order of battle. Our photograph shows the aircraft and crew situation as it was on March 21, 1945, when Bomber Command was almost at its peak strength.
[*Flight International*

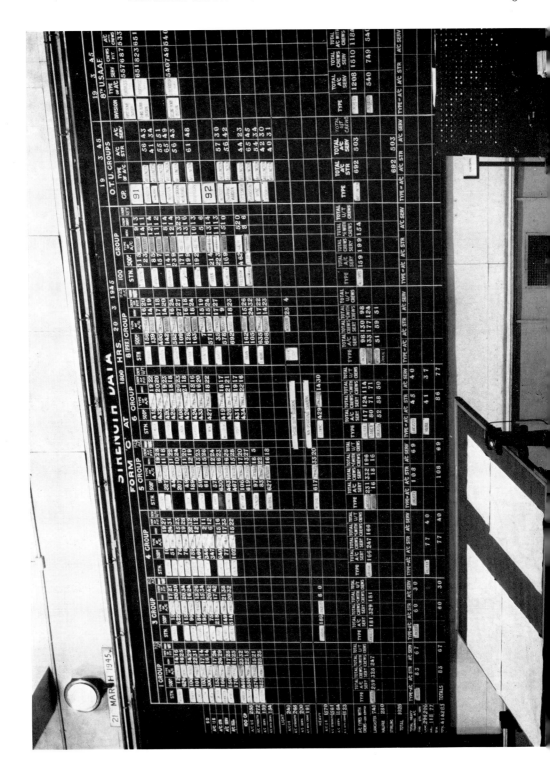

The Rhine crossing. Part of the airborne armada prepares for take-off from Tarrant Rushton, Dorset, for Germany on March 24, 1945. In the centre of the runway are Hamilcar gliders; flanking them are their Halifax tugs. The entire Anglo-U.S. aerial armada comprised 4,616 powered aircraft (including fighter escort) and 1,326 gliders, a total of 5,942 aircraft.   [I.W.M.

Fitters at work on a Liberator of Transport Command's South Atlantic ferry service at Windsor Field, Nassau, in the Bahamas. The Liberators ran a scheduled passenger and freight service back and forth from Florida and the Bahamas to the Gold Coast, a distance of over 3,000 miles. One of them, piloted by Capt Norman Williams, once made four crossings from Brazil to the Gold Coast and back in three days, sixteen-and-a-half hours. To do this, the crew travelled 11,500 miles in $88\frac{1}{2}$ hours, which is an average of about 135 m.p.h. for nearly four days. In the course of the trips they had breakfast in Ascension Island on four consecutive mornings, 'so that the inhabitants thought we were nuts'.   [I.W.M.

Roughing it. Passengers in a Liberator of Transport Command during a flight from Dorval, Montreal, to Goose Bay, Alaska. [*I.W.M.*

Bomb damage to the mighty Krupps armament empire at Essen, photographed by a Mosquito of 2nd T.A.F. just after VE-Day. The works occupied an area of 2½ miles by 1,500 yards, and were severely damaged by Bomber Command many times during the war, but up to 1944 were repaired by the enemy just as frequently. After a particularly heavy raid in October 1944, however, all production virtually ceased and the works remained out of action for the rest of the war.

[*I.W.M.*

Damage to the Blohm and Voss aircraft factory near Hamburg caused by R.A.F. bombing. In the main building, rows of 50 aircraft—including the Messerschmitt Bf 109Gs shown—were destroyed when the roof fell on them. On the edge of the adjoining airfield was a wired-in camp for the slave labour employed at the factory.

First British troops to land in Denmark early in May 1945 were some of our airborne troops fresh from their race across Germany to link up with the Russians. Here, crowds who have broken through the barrier at Kastrup airfield, Copenhagen, carry airborne troops shoulder high from their Dakota aircraft. *[I.W.M.*

Operation *Exodus*. When Bomber Command's offensive ceased, crews turned to happier tasks, including that of repatriating ex prisoners-of-war. In this scene, taken on VE-Day—May 8 1945—F/Sgt. J. P. Beesley is welcomed home by a senior officer after flying back to the U.K. in a Lancaster of No. 97 Squadron, from Coningsby, Lincs.

[*I.W.M.*

After VE-Day, aircraft of Coastal Command continued to escort convoys as a precautionary measure against any U-boats that might not have surrendered. Final convoy patrol was carried out by Wg Cdr. J. Barrett and crew of No. 201 Squadron, in Sunderland V ML778 'Z-for-Zebra', and this historic occasion is recorded below.

[*I.W.M.*

Some war winners on show on the site of D. H. Evans's bombed store in Oxford Street, London, on the occasion of 'Britain's Aircraft' Exhibition in June 1945. In the foreground is the veteran Halifax III LV907 'Friday the 13th' which flew 128 operations with No. 158 Squadron from Lissett, Yorks. Also visible in the picture are a Beaufighter, a naval Firefly, a Tempest, and an Army Auster.

Skies of Freedom. Spitfires lead the Victory fly-past over London in 1945.

SOUTH-EAST ASIA

Vildebeestes over Singapore Harbour. This is a pre-war scene, but illustrates the type of aircraft used by the Singapore-based Nos. 36 and 100 Squadrons in their gallant but hopeless struggle against the invading Japanese in 1941. Both units were decimated, although two Vildebeestes of 36 Squadron fought on in Java until March 1942, when they were lost in Sumatra whilst attempting to reach Burma.

Blenheims over Akyab during a low-level attack on Japanese shipping in the harbour. Although obsolescent, the Blenheims remained in first-line service in Burma until late 1943. In their latter days, spares were virtually unobtainable; but in the case of No. 11 Squadron—and this applied no doubt to the others, too—spirits remained high and it was said that the veteran Blenheims flew on happiness alone. So famous did the comradeship of the crews become in India that men tried to get themselves posted to the Blenheims, despite the maturity of the aircraft. [*I.W.M.*

Brewster Buffalo fighters and a No. 62 Squadron Blenheim I at Singapore in late 1941 before the Japanese invasion. Both types were outclassed by their Jap counterparts, the Zero fighters and Mitsubishi bombers.   [*I.W.M.*

Wellington X of No. 99 Squadron at an airfield in Burma during the seige of Imphal. At that time the Wimpys undertook the emergency transport task of ferrying 250-lb bombs to the Hurri-bomber squadrons operating against the Tiddim—Imphal road from airfields on the Imphal Plain.   [*I.W.M.*

Under the command of Brigadier (later Major-General) Charles Orde Wingate, a small force of British troops known as the Long Range Penetration Group, or Chindits, to give them another of their official names, several times penetrated deep behind Japanese lines in Burma, destroying supply dumps, cutting communications and inflicting heavy losses on the enemy. Frequently they were without food and lived on whatever they could find until supplies arrived, dropped from R.A.F. aircraft by parachute into jungle clearings. Picture shows a Dakota on a landing ground in enemy-occupied Burma, waiting to evacuate sick and wounded Chindits towards the end of the first three-months long Chindit expedition in June 1943.

Hurri-bomber attacks a bridge on the Tiddim Road in 1944. When the Japanese Fifteenth Army in Manipur, India, was retreating down the Tiddim and Tamu roads during the monsoon of 1944, the R.A.F.'s Hurri-bombers attacked the enemy remorselessly, shooting up his bunker positions, hideouts, and transport, and strafing troops on the move. During the fighting along the road to Kalemyo, where the forty hairpin bends winding down the mountainside were known as the 'Chocolate Staircase', the Hurri-bombers literally went from milestone to milestone, obliterating enemy pockets of resistance and so easing the progress of our troops. [*I.W.M.*

Vultee Vengeance dive-bomber returns to a forward airfield after a successful sortie against Japanese positions in Burma. Four R.A.F. squadrons flew Vengeances in Burma and, after an inauspicious start due to teething troubles, the type became a most successful and accurate attack aircraft. Pin-point targets just in front of our own troops were bombed and strafed with uncanny accuracy and, following one attack at Maungdaw, observers reported that: 'After bombing, six funeral pyres were seen'. On another occasion they noted with grim satisfaction that 'six lorry loads of dead were removed from Razabil'. [*I.W.M.*

This field kitchen in Burma was made from used 40-gallon petrol cans, biscuit tins and mud. It took about three hours to build and is being used by Cpl. A. Clarke of Aberdeen.   [*I.W.M.*

Left: Monsoo⌐ weather in Burm⌐ This scene on forward airstri⌐ shows Cpl. A. ⌐ Toon (centre) ar⌐ L.A.C. R. Coghla⌐ (right) pulling trolley with a 500-l⌐ American - typ⌐ bomb for a Spitfir⌐ L.F.VIII of No. 60 Squadron. Pushin⌐ the bomb is L.A.C⌐ R. Judd.   [*I.W.M.*

Below: Beaufighte⌐ stands at its disper⌐ sal on a forwar⌐ airstrip on th⌐ Mandalay front i⌐ Burma while groun⌐ crew crowd roun⌐ the pilot who ha⌐ just returned fro⌐ a mission ove⌐ Japanese-hel⌐ territory. Beau⌐ fighters first arrive⌐ in the Far Eas⌐ theatre—for th⌐ defence of Calcutt⌐ —in January 1943⌐ and subsequent re⌐ inforcements o⌐ Beaus proved of th⌐ greatest use i⌐ offensive opera⌐ tions. Their lon⌐ range enabled the⌐ to penetrate dee⌐ into Burma, an⌐ they were able t⌐ bring heavy fire⌐ power to bear o⌐ targets such as rive⌐ craft, locomotive⌐ and mechanica⌐ transport. The fast⌐ near-silent ap⌐ proach of th⌐ ground - strafin⌐ Beaufighters of Ai⌐ Command, South-⌐ East Asia, earne⌐ them the nicknam⌐ of 'Whispering⌐ Death'.   [*I.W.M.*

Liberators of No. 99 Squadron bomb a Japanese airfield near Rangoon. Thanks to the skill of the C.O. of one of Strategic Air Force's R.A.F. Liberator squadrons—Wing Cdr. J. Blackburn of No. 159 Squadron—who conducted experiments in fuel consumption, Liberators were able to reach Bangkok— 1,100 miles from their bases in Bengal—each carrying 8,000lb of bombs. This vast improvement in efficiency was commended by the Americans and the example was followed throughout Strategic Air Force. Gradually it became possible for the bombers to make round trips of 2,300 miles to the Kra Isthmus and 2,800 miles to the Malay Peninsula. On several occasions Penang harbour was mined in sorties which involved round trips of more than 3,000 miles, and 18 hours of flying over the sea. [I.W.M

Above: Thunderbolts set off to attack enemy communications and airstrips in Burma, watched by ground crew servicing an aircraft and by their fellow pilots who are waiting at readiness on this forward airstrip. From late 1944, when they first became operational in Burma, R.A.F. Thunderbolts flew 'cab-rank' patrols directed by ground—and sometimes airborne—visual posts. With their three 500-lb bombs and eight 0.50-calibre guns, they played havoc among Japanese troops and supply lines. [*I.W.M.*

Opposite: R.A.F. Thunderbolt pilot, Sgt. R. Standish Walker of No. 135 Squadron, dressed in his 'Beadon' flying suit, complete with jungle kit, Mae West, knives and screwdrivers, climbs into his aircraft while L.A.C. R. Rainford, a member of the ground crew, stands by. [*I.W.M.*

Below: Burma-based Thunderbolt 'Jungle Queen' is bombed up with a 500-pounder by L.A.C. Rich, A.C. C. G. Cox, L.A.C. R. J. Dunnings and A.C. E. J. Price, Christmas 1944. [*I.W.M.*

Above: 'It's one of ours'. R.A.F. Regiment personnel manning an anti-aircraft gun on the Arakan front in Burma, give a wave to a Hurricane pilot as he returns to base from a patrol.   [*I.W.M.*

Opposite. One of the main tasks of the Liberators—R.A.F. and U.S.A.A.F.—of Strategic Air Force in Burma was that of cutting, at long range, the enemy's supply routes. Targets were some 5,000 miles of railways and, particularly, the infamous Siam-Burma railway linking Bangkok with Moulmein, which had been built at a cost of the lives of 24,000 Allied prisoners-of-war. As there were only a few large targets, the Liberators concentrated on destroying bridges and obliterating tracks, and our picture shows an R.A.F. machine flying over the wreckage of a 200-ft bridge that had been destroyed by 1,000-lb bombs.   [*I.W.M.*

R.A.F. Salvage Unit retrieves a crashed Hurricane in Burma. Hurricanes did splendid work in that theatre, one particularly remarkable operation taking place near Myinmu in mid-February 1945, during the final Allied offensive. Here the enemy had concentrated most of his precious tanks and, with great cunning, had concealed them in what appeared to be small native huts, camouflaged with the boughs of trees. One pilot, his suspicions aroused, ripped off the roof of one hut with gunfire to reveal a tank. Other Hurricanes soon joined in and 12 tanks were quickly uncovered and destroyed. This feat brought an exuberant signal from a nearby British Division: 'Nippon Hardware Corporation has gone bust. Nice work. Tanks a million'.   [*I.W.M.*

Supply train caught by Beaufighter cannon-fire among the trees near Kanbalu, Burma.   [*I.W.M.*

Dakota drops supplies by parachute to troops of the Fourteenth Army on a bridgehead south of the Irawaddy River in central Burma early in 1945.

[*I.W.M.*

Ground crews of an R.A.F. squadron operating on the Arakan front, in Burma, unload a Stinson L-5 Sentinel liaison aircraft from an LCV in 1945. L-5s were used extensively on the Mandalay and Arakan fronts in Burma for transporting wounded from the fighting zones to forward clearing stations, whence men were flown back to base hospitals.
[*I.W.M.*

Armourers carry a rocket to a Hurricane on an advanced airstrip in Central Burma early in 1945. They are L.A.C. J. Grogan of Manchester and (right) L.A.C. C. Foster of Blackpool.
[*I.W.M·*

Hurricane being prepared for an armed reconnaissance sortie in Burma early in 1945. Cpl. E. Yeo (left) of Dunton Green, Sevenoaks, Kent, and L.A.C. C. E. Bland of South Norwood, London, load the 20-mm cannon with shells; while in the background L.A.C. D. L. Worthington of Manchester and L.A.C. E. H. Davey of Sundridge Park, Kent, install the camera.   [*I.W.M.*

Above: Mosquito aircraft operating from the Arakan and elsewhere in Burma did a magnificent job in the Burma campaign in support of the 14th Army. They attacked Japanese strong points, infantry and motor transport, and flew many photographic reconnaissance sorties. Here L.A.C. C. Driver of Attleborough, Norfolk, watches a Mosquito ·F.B.VI taxi out for take-off at an airfield in the Arakan in 1945.
                                                                        [*I.W.M.*

Above: Catalina returns to its base in Ceylon after a long ocean patrol. R.A.F. Catalina and Sunderland flying-boats operating from Ceylon flew over Allied convoys and shipping lanes night and day, to protect them from Japanese surface and submarine attacks. In the course of their duty, the crews had to fly long distances out to sea, sometimes through extremely severe tropical weather conditions. [*I.W.M.*

Left: Catalina comes up the slipway for a maintenance check at Korangi Creek, Karachi. This base—one of the largest of its kind in India—did most of the maintenance work on R.A.F. Catalinas and Sunderlands in that area, and it was from there that such aircraft were routed on to their forward bases. R.A.F. flying-boats played many and diverse roles during the war in South-East Asia. In addition to anti-submarine and shipping patrols, shadowing of Japanese naval task forces, bombing of vital targets, and ferrying sick and wounded, R.A.F. Catalinas took part in anti-locust patrols, making daily sorties over the mountains and deserts of Baluchistan and across the Persian border to check and destroy the breeding places of the locust pests which constitute a great menace to agriculture in North-West India. [*I.W.M.*

Spitfire VIIIs of No. 136 Squadron, top-scoring fighter squadron in S.E.A.C. with 100 kills and 150 probables and damaged, during preparations for Operation *Zipper*—the invasion of Malaya, which the atomic bomb made unnecessary. In the background are Liberators of No. 99 Squadron. [*I.W.M.*